THREE-STEP
TRAY TASKING

Logic & Critical Thinking Activities
for Young Children

Join us on the web at

EarlyChildEd.delmar.com

THREE-STEP TRAY TASKING

Logic & Critical Thinking Activities for Young Children

Victoria Folds, Ed.D.

THOMSON

━━━

DELMAR LEARNING   Australia   Canada   Mexico   Singapore   Spain   United Kingdom   United States

Three-Step Tray Tasking: Logic & Critical Thinking Activities For Young Children

Victoria Folds, Ed.D.

Vice President, Career Education Strategic Business Unit:
Dawn Gerrain

Director of Learning Solutions:
John Fedor

Managing Editor:
Robert L. Serenka, Jr.

Senior Acquisitions Editor:
Erin O'Connor

Product Manager:
Philip Mandl

Editorial Assistant:
Alison Archambault

Director of Production:
Wendy A. Troeger

Production Manager:
Mark Bernard

Content Project Manager:
Jeffrey Varecka

Art Director:
Joy Kocsis

Compositor:
Newgen

Illustrator:
Patricia Knight

Director of Marketing:
Wendy E. Mapstone

Channel Manager:
Kristin McNary

Marketing Coordinator:
Scott A. Chrysler

Marketing Specialist:
Erica S. Conley

Cover Design:
Joseph Villanova

Interior Design:
Judi Orozco

Library of Congress Cataloging-in-Publication Data

Folds, Victoria.
  Three-step tray tasking : logic & critical thinking activities for young children / Victoria Folds. — 1st ed.
     p. cm.
  Includes bibliographical references.
  ISBN 978-1-4180-5296-6 (alk. paper)
  1. Early childhood education—Activity programs. 2. Education, Preschool—Activity programs.
  3. Creative activities and seat work.
  I. Title.
  LB1139.35.A37F65 2008
  372.21—dc22

                         2007010620

NOTICE TO THE READER

Contents

My heartfelt appreciation to my husband Charlie for his patient photography skill for all the photos. Thanks to my daughter Jennifer for her valuable input on this project. I also dedicate this book to my daughter Abbie and son Joshua along with my six grandsons who keep me energized and focused!

Special thanks go to Children's World and Mrs. Mary Lou Raham for letting us shoot photos of children at her center.

Preface

WHAT IS *THREE-STEP TRAY TASKING?*

Three-Step Tray Tasking, the second in a series of Tray Tasking books, encourages the development of children's organizational thinking skills through concrete, hands-on tasks. *Three-Step Tray Tasking* is written for early childhood educators and families with young children ages four years old and up. The intention is to provide readers with innovative methods to increase a child's ability to develop organized thinking habits. Many times teachers and parents assume that organizational thinking is something children already possess. However, many young children are disorganized in their early thinking, and teachers often mistake this for a lack of motivation or avoidance to begin or complete an activity. Often the seeming lack of motivation or avoidance is caused by disorganized thinking itself. Weak organizational abilities may be an obstacle to a child's learning and may in fact, result in a lowering of motivation. Displaying disorganized thinking patterns may cause a lower threshold of success for bright students and be an underlying cause of emotional distress in otherwise emotionally healthy children.

I've been in early childhood education for over 30 years, and during that time, I have observed young children who don't know where to start or what to do next. They are not able to make a plan or anticipate an outcome. I have watched the disorganized child pause at the beginning of child choice time trying to decide what to do and often spend his or her time moving from one activity to another without completing any of them. Frequently this child would wait for the teacher to direct him or her to an activity or the child would never make a choice, often becoming sad or agitated. Offering an ordered, planned activity choice provides a child with a sensible solution that he or she could control and complete. These activities do not detract from the child choice philosophy endorsed by the National Association for the Education of Young Children (NAEYC), but rather offer the child an opportunity to increase concentration and focus on specific actions to complete a task.

GOALS OF *THREE-STEP TRAY TASKING*

Three-Step Tray Tasking offers children activities to reinforce critical thinking skills while appealing to their learning modalities, or distinct styles of learning. Different learning styles are enhanced as children engage in each tray task. The visual learner perceives a sense of an object by seeing the teacher display materials used in a game or activity, such as the clues on each tray, to organize his or her thinking ability. The auditory learner channels information through hearing the teacher's instructions as a task is presented. The kinesthetic, or hands-on learner manipulates the tools on each tray that offer sensory stimulation as he or she focuses on completing a task. In agreement with NAEYC, which concludes that young children are active learners, we can assume that many prefer hands-on learning as their learning style of choice.

As a child completes a task, he or she employs many emerging abilities such as sequencing; time concepts of beginning, middle, and end; logical progression; and attending to a task until completion. The child is classifying actions, categorizing steps, and following directions. For the child who is building his or her organizational thinking, these tasks are valuable because they provide the teaching of these skills through the manipulation of the materials as the child becomes actively involved at each step along the way. The use of the specific tools and materials builds fine motor strength in arm, wrist, hand, and finger muscles, promotes eye/hand coordination and strengthens left-to-right and top-to-bottom progression. Children are making decisions, problem solving, and increasing their awareness of their thinking processes which provide a sense of control. Children are also increasing the ability to follow complex instructions when using *Three-Step Tray Tasking.*

Three-Step Tray Tasking serves as a teacher resource for designing an organizational climate for young children. The materials identified are common, everyday tools that are already found in the classroom used in a sequential format. *Three-Step Tray Tasking* provides a logical, planned way for children to experience following directions at their own pace.

Teachers often seek suggestions on how to help children follow directions, sequence events, and complete tasks. Teachers often assume these essential skills as children are observed using traditional classroom materials. *Three-Step Tray Tasking* provides tangible tasks for observing, recording, and documenting growth over time.

Tasks are intended to be child driven. A teacher assembles the three trays and may demonstrate the outcome to the children at circle time or other small group setting. However, a child elects to complete the tray task on his or her own. Teachers provide a "Sign In" sheet next to the activity for children to write their name to show they have chosen the task. This will help the teacher identify who is completing a task and prompts the teacher to complete the observation chart for each child.

Children not only practice skills needed in kindergarten they experience the opportunity to begin, continue, and complete a task that is enjoyable and fun. Children learn by doing and *Three-Step Tray Task-*

ing provides affordable, hands-on tasks that take only minutes to set up and provides teachers with a multitude of observable traits when assessing each child.

HOW THIS BOOK IS ORGANIZED

The table of contents lists the chapters and sections of this book. The chapters containing tasks follow a logical pattern:

1. **First Tray Step:** The first tray indicates the initial actions that begin the three-step process. It's a signal to the child to begin. It requires tracing of a shape or object.

2. **Second Tray Step:** The next tray is the middle, or second step and combines work from the first tray with a new action. This step requires the child to cut the traced shape or object.

3. **Third Tray Step:** The third, or end step signals a final action to complete the goal of the task. This step requires compiling materials using glue, tape, or other means of connection. This is the assemblage stage.

Each task instruction follows a similar sequence:

- **Materials** – Lists the necessary items needed to successfully complete each task. It provides readers a way to prepare the task.
    - The size of the construction paper should fit the tray unless otherwise stated.
- **Setup** – Details the placement of the trays and what is placed on each tray. This is an important step so that the child will see the sequencing concept by what is placed on each tray.
- **Task** – The task itself is written in a beginning, middle, and end format. Each part begins with "The goal . . ." so that teachers and families will keep in mind the purpose of each action a child encounters.
- **Outcome** – A stated outcome is the achievement of the goals. It is what the child should be able to accomplish as a result of following the goals.
- **Emerging Skills** – The emerging skills are the result of the actions while doing the task. Each task provides a child with an opportunity to repeat movements and motions that become

the habit or routine of the tasks. Children will emerge with different levels of skills depending on their own experiences and ages.

- **Extension Activity** – Many of the tasks have suggested extension activities that provide further enhancements of the task's purpose. They are also a way for a teacher to challenge a higher-level thinking child.

 The Online Companion to accompany *Three-Step Tray Tasking* contains teacher stencils. Each task is noted on the page for you to create cardboard or manila stock stencils as well as paper labels for some of the tasks. Use the paper stencils as your guide. You may wish to make your own stencils to coincide with your theme or unit emphasis, or you may want to purchase ready-made ones.

Please read the entire task before copying the stencils so you will know if you need multiple copies of each of the pages. Some tasks are not listed as they do not require a stencil. It is recommended that you purchase or use existing uppercase and lowercase letter stencils to complement the manuscript style in your local school system.

The Online Companion can be found at www.earlychilded.delmar.com.

INTENDED USERS OF *THREE-STEP TRAY TASKING*

Early childhood teachers and parents of pre-kindergarten and kindergarten age children benefit from the contents of the book. Families may use these tasks as one-on-one time focusing on the emerging skills needed for a successful kindergarten experience. The tasks are easily set up at home in an area where older children in the family may be doing their homework. They can also be set up in a designated area of the kitchen or the child's bedroom. The tools, paper, and trays may be placed in a storage container until ready for use. For classrooms, one preschool child at a time uses the three-step tray task displayed by the teacher. The task is set up in the classroom as an independent work area. Children may choose to complete the task during child choice time.

Each task in this book is accompanied with pictures that show each step of a task. Each task contains three pictures to represent a beginning, middle, and end. If a teacher or parent chooses to use tasks from different sections of the book, the three pictures are always included so users won't have to rely on memory to know how each tray is prepared.

It is my expectation that as these tasks are completed, children develop intrinsic motivation to enhance emerging organization thinking and enjoy completing a tray task.

ACKNOWLEDGEMENTS

The editors at Thomson Delmar Learning and the author thank the following reviewers for their time, effort, and thoughtful contributions that helped shape the final text.

Jody Martin
Director of Education & Training for Crème de la Crème, Inc.
Greenwood Village, CO

Lisa Thomas
Jack London Middle School
Wheeling, IL

Patricia Capistron
Lead Teacher, Rocking Unicorn Nursery School
West Chatham, MA

Katherine M. Lozano
Executive Director, Blessed Sacrament Academy Child Development Center
San Antonio, TX

Lynnette McCarty
President, The National Association of Child Care Professionals, and Executive Director of Serendipity Children's Center
Tumwater, WA

Linda Rivers
Director of the University of Tennessee at Chattanooga Child Care Center & Learning Lab
Chattanooga, TN

Dawn Hove
University of Nebraska at Omaha Child Care Center
Omaha, NE

Introduction

WHAT KINDERGARTEN TEACHERS ARE SAYING

When interviewing kindergarten teachers, I always ask for a list of attributes they think entering kindergarten children should possess. The lists always include references to organizational abilities. The abilities center on developing thinking skills such as:

- identifying and describing sequences of objects or events
- using information learned in various experiences to solve problems
- following complex instructions
- increasing vocabulary for describing complex observations
- copying simple letters, patterns, and shapes
- cutting, placing, and pasting project work
- tracing around and inside
- assuming independent responsibilities for completing tasks
- indicating a willingness to attempt more difficult tasks by attending to tasks for increasingly longer periods of time

This book addresses many of the organizational abilities noted by kindergarten teachers for the preschool and kindergarten student. Young children should have opportunities to identify and describe sequences of objects or events. When identifying events, they use information learned in various experiences to solve problems.

Many kindergarten teachers ask for children to enter kindergarten with an understanding of how to cut, place, and paste project work through the copying of simple letters, patterns, and shapes. This ability does not take the place of process art, the open-ended art experience approach that is advocated by early childhood educators; rather, it is a learning center unto itself. The ability to trace, cut, and paste is referred to as assemblage. Through the assembling of materials, young children assume independent responsibilities for completing each task which may indicate a willingness to attempt more difficult tasks based on their accomplishment level. Assembling differs from open-ended art by having a child complete a task for a specific end product. In open-ended art, a child creatively expresses himself or herself without the requirements that the end product look like a pattern or teacher example.

Organizational abilities in young children develop through structure in the learning environment and the processing of information as they mature. This tells us that an organized classroom plays a vital role in the ability of a child to gain clues as he or she builds thinking abilities. Children look for consistencies in the environment that reinforce dependability and security. If the puzzle was on the shelf yesterday, the child assumes the puzzle will be on the shelf today; a fact they begin to depend upon. The mainstay of children's security is that there is little change in the people and routine of the classroom. Children grow to rely on familiar room arrangements, familiar faces, and similarities in day-to-day events. These constants form a framework of predictability that allows a child to explore, discover, and investigate. As children engage in daily exploration and discovery in the learning areas, they reassure their thoughts and construct knowledge. Routines in the classroom also play a significant role in the organization of the day. Children rely on similar daily experiences provided during the same time frame which hold the potential for new learning outcomes. As children progress through routines, they continually add new information to their short-term memory which begins to extend into long-term application. Teachers motivate children to learn through organized learning experiences which lead children to regulate their own thinking. Teachers should not just tell children what they are to learn, but rather design developmentally appropriate activities that allow children to respond to concrete materials and thus develop conceptual skills. Early childhood teachers are concept builders, not content builders. They set the stage for the learning process through hands-on activities that foster an understanding of the world and how it works.

Many kindergarten teachers I have interviewed also respond with suggested non-academic skills that are useful for transitioning into kindergarten. These skills are correlated to core values as defined by the NAEYC national standards for early childhood.

1. Playing and Working Independently and Collaboratively

- Plays and works appropriately with and without peers
- Stays with an activity for an appropriate amount of time
- Plays and works with minimal prompts from the teacher

Three-Step Tray Tasking promotes working independently and staying on task by providing hands-on experiences that progress from one stage of assembling to the next until the task is completed.

2. Following Directions

- Responds to adults' questions
- Responds appropriately to multi-step verbal directions
- Responds appropriately to verbal directions that include common school-related prepo-

sitions such as on-off, up-down, in-out, etc., nouns, and verbs
- Modifies behavior as needed when given verbal feedback
- Recalls and follows directions for tasks previously discussed or demonstrated
- Watches others or seeks help if he or she does not understand directions

Three-Step Tray Tasking offers children the opportunity to hear directions about a task and rely on short-term memory to work through the task by using auditory, visual, and kinesthetic clues within each task.

3. Responding to Routines

- Learns new routines after limited practice
- Moves quickly and quietly from one activity to another without individual reminders

Three-Step Tray Tasking engages young children in a beginning, middle, and end routine that allows for a comfort level of familiarity while using varied tools to achieve each task goal. *Three-Step Tray Tasking* acts as a learning center which provides many opportunities for repetition of actions.

By referring to these characteristics as young children's internal thinking skills we begin to see the need to provide activities so that pre-kindergarten and kindergarten children implement organizational learning processes.

This book provides simple tasks that encourage children to use eye/hand coordination and higher level thinking as they work through three steps that provide a logically planned beginning, middle, and end to a task.

It is recommended that teachers read through the book to choose tasks that fit into the current curriculum needs of the classroom and the needs of the children.

THEORISTS: THEIR THOUGHTS AND *THREE-STEP TRAY TASKING*

Howard Gardner, a current theorist, provides a new view of intelligence. He suggests at least eight distinct types of intelligence. This theory, referred to as the Theory of Multiple Intelligences or MI Theory, has encouraged many to rethink ways in which learning takes place and the ways in which we measure intelligence. One of his identified intelligences is that of Bodily-Kinesthetic Intelligence; the ability of the body to control movement using both hemispheres of the brain while strengthening the dexterity of the dominating side. Gardner identifies the ability to move the body in meaningful coordinated ways as an example of intelligence. His theory prompts us to realize that young children enter our classrooms with many different skills and talents, and we need to recognize and respect these varying abilities.

Another theorist, Maria Montessori, developed a hypothesis that practical strategies play a very significant role in the learning process. She concluded that children pass through sensitive periods of learning throughout their childhood and on into adulthood. During these sensitive periods, children are eager and able to master certain tasks. She also promoted the idea that to fully develop the intellect a child must have physical activity. Montessori felt that learning is accomplished through doing. *Three-Step Tray Tasking* provides the opportunity for young children to move through three sequential stages of an activity using physical as well as thinking abilities.

Lev Vygotsky, a noted philosopher provided us with insight as to what he coined the zone of proximal development or ZPD. His concept explains that there exists a gap between a child's independent performance of a task and his or her ability to perform a task with the help of an adult or peer. Therefore, there is an area or a gap in which an observant teacher must determine when to offer help and when to encourage a child to work independently. As with *Three-Step Tray Tasking*, a child builds knowledge by processing through a task but has the assurance of assistance if needed.

Erik Erikson's assumption of human development supports the need for children to engage in meaningful tasks. The preschool and kindergarten child is developing a sense of initiative by making plans, setting goals, and working hard to accomplish tasks. Erikson's theory positions this strong urge to be in conflict with guilt or a feeling of not being able to accomplish a task. Teachers assist children with successful ways to overcome this psychosocial crisis. *Three-Step Tray Tasking* provides ways to demonstrate trustworthiness, allow independence, and encourage the planning and exploration needed to accomplish a task.

Jean Piaget, a well-known theorist, concludes that intellectual, or cognitive development has sev-

eral stages. He identifies preoperational intelligence as the stage in the preschool years when young children are exploring their effects on the environment by discovery, exploration, and manipulation. By focusing on the period of processing from preoperational intelligence to concrete operations, we see that preschool and kindergarten children begin to use symbolic thinking rather than learn only through sensory and motor interactions. Because children are still in an egocentric period of development, they see things only from their own perspective. Children passing through this stage of development begin to attempt to master logical thinking but need tools designed to support the journey. *Three-Step Tray Tasking* provides a logical sequencing of tasks that invite a child to work through a series of steps to complete purposeful actions in circumstances that require critical thinking and consequences.

One way in which Piaget explains intellectual knowledge is through the use of the terms *assimilation* and *accommodation*. To assimilate is to absorb or experience new information. To accommodate the new information is to make room for it through a process of changing what was known and including the new information to form a new base of knowledge. These words represent the processes responsible for the change from sensorimotor schemata to cognitive schemata. A schema (plural is schemata) is a collection of distinct but similar action sequences. "Every scheme is . . . coordinated with all other schemata and itself constitutes a totality with differentiated parts" (Piaget, *The Origins of Intelligence in Children*, 1952, p. 7). Assimilation is the cognitive process by which a person integrates new perceptual, motor, or conceptual matter into existing schemata or patterns of behavior. In other words, children experience something new and accommodate that new information by assimilating or absorbing the information to form new knowledge. This identifies a constant process of learning; discovering today's knowledge, storing it in the brain in short-term memory, then discovering something new about that knowledge tomorrow and expanding the original information to make way for more knowledge. Once accommodation has taken place, a child will begin to use the newfound knowledge in similar or new ways. The child conceptualizes newly learned knowledge in his or her own way, thus this book's references of the different modalities or learning styles.

The processes of assimilation and accommodation are necessary for cognitive growth and development. As children mature, they reach a balance between assimilation and accommodation which is referred to by Piaget as *equilibration*. It's a self-regulatory mechanism necessary to ensure the developing child's efficient interaction with the environment (Wadsworth, *Piaget's Theory of Cognitive and Affective Development*, 1989, pp. 16–17). Mental activity combined with physical activity is vital as children construct their own systems of knowledge as they progress toward becoming competent thinkers. It is the goal of *Three-Step Tray Tasking* to offer children an opportunity to reach equilibration.

Chapter 1

How to Organize
a Tray Task Area

Three-Step Tray Tasking promotes organizational thinking skills by offering tasks that are organized in a beginning, middle, and ending sequence. Three trays provide a concrete way to show the first, second, and third steps necessary to complete each task. Teachers set up the three trays with visual clues as to each tray's function. A child is encouraged to follow the trays by "walking through" the three tray process which involves not only thinking, but also moving the body along the sequence to reinforce the movement from left to right—one of the directions for emerging reading and writing skills.

⁂ HOW TO ORGANIZE A THREE-STEP TRAY TASKING AREA

The adult's job is to set up a tray tasking area where one child at a time may engage in purposeful work. A low shelf or table is recommended where a child stands in front of the trays so that he or she may move the body along the tray sequence. Trays should be placed next to one another in a horizontal line. Each tray represents the same purpose for every task. The first tray is always the tracing or drawing tray. The second tray is always the cutting tray. Finally, the third tray is always the assemblage tray using glue, a single hole punch, and yarn or ribbon according to the goal of the task. The positioning of the materials on the tray is significant as a pencil is positioned at the top or left side of the tray, the scissors at the top of a tray, and the glue stick at the top of the tray thus involving the child in top-to-bottom and left-to-right progression as they work. As children use each of the items, they develop an emerging ability to hold a pencil for writing and strengthen the eyes for reading.

Three-Step Tray Tasking is designed to be used as a child choice. The teacher uses small group time to explain the purpose of a tray task; introduce the concept of beginning, middle, and end; and then demonstrate the tools to be used as well as the expected outcome. A task may be available for children to access until all have had a turn or until the teacher wishes to introduce a different one. Observing each child's abilities when attempting and completing each step of the task provides teachers with information about how the child approaches a task, takes control of him or herself during the task, and if the task is completed according to an anticipated outcome. It is recommended that tray tasking become its own learning area. The very positioning of the trays suggests to a visual learner a logical flow of actions that results in a goal or completed task. A visual learner will associate the arrangement of trays as providing picture clues as to its purpose. The materials displayed on each tray will also indicate the movement from one tray to the next. The auditory learner will gather clues from the teacher's instructions for each stage of the task. The kinesthetic, or hands-on, learner gains understanding as he or she engages in meaningful, tactile, and skill-building activities to accomplish each task. Many of the tasks revolve around using pencils, scissors, and other tools to promote eye/hand coordination, fine motor skills, and the development of organizational thinking skills. The materials suggested are those already in classrooms but not necessarily used as in the *Three-Step Tray Tasking* method.

To be specific, the materials will include many of the following tools found in the early childhood classroom:

- paper
- stencils (teacher-made, resources from book, or store-bought)
- scissors
- pencils
- colored pencils
- chalk
- markers
- ruler
- hole punch
- yarn
- ribbon
- glue
- tape

When a child chooses to complete a task, he or she needs limited distractions to be able to concentrate. By visually setting up a learning area where a child sees three trays, side-by-side he or she progresses from tray to tray, follows directions, assembles, and completes a task in a sequential order.

After a child completes a task, he or she returns the non-consumable materials to their original tray positions and places paper on the first tray for the next person. Teachers may place the appropriate paper in a basket or bin conveniently located close to the tray tasking activity.

OBSERVATION AND RECORDING

A Three-Step Tray Tasking Classroom Chart, found in this section, shows how to set up a classroom chart to easily document tasks. Fill in selected tasks across the top columns and write children's names down the first column. Attach this chart to a clipboard or post by the learning area.

The chart assists in the observation of the children's ability to complete tasks successfully. You may transfer markings to each child's individual charts when convenient. Teachers choose tasks based on the children's abilities as well as incorporating monthly skill emphases.

Make copies of the chart as you expand the number of tasks completed.

THREE-STEP TRAY TASKING CLASSROOM CHART

CHILD'S NAME	TASKS							
1.								
2.								
3.								
4.								
5.								
6.								
7.								
8.								
9.								
10.								
11.								
12.								

Suggested symbols to make your checking go faster:

✔ Completed Task
WTH With Teacher's Help
_____ Leave space blank if child needs another opportunity to succeed

INDIVIDUAL CHILD THREE-STEP TRAY TASK CHART

Child's Name _____ Age _____

THREE-STEP TRAY TASK	GOOD JOB	WITH HELP	NOT YET	COMMENTS
SHAPE—TRACE, CUT, AND ASSEMBLE				
1. Circle Shape				
2. Oval Shape				
3. Crescent Shape				
4. Square Shape				
5. Rectangle Shape				
6. Triangle Shape				
7. Diamond Shape				
8. Pentagon Shape				
9. Hexagon Shape				
10. Octagon Shape				
SIZE—TRACE OR DRAW, CUT, AND ASSEMBLE				
11. Small, Medium, and Large Circles				
12. Small, Medium, and Large Ovals				
13. Small, Medium, and Large Crescents				
14. Small, Medium, and Large Squares				
15. Small, Medium, and Large Rectangles				
16. Small, Medium, and Large Triangles				
17. Small, Medium, and Large Diamonds				
18. Small, Medium, and Large Pentagons				
19. Small, Medium, and Large Hexagons				
20. Small, Medium, and Large Octagons				

(continues)

THREE-STEP TRAY TASK	GOOD JOB	WITH HELP	NOT YET	COMMENTS
PARTS TO A WHOLE—TRACE, CUT, AND ASSEMBLE				
21. Two Pieces Make a Whole				
22. Three Pieces Make a Whole				
23. Four Pieces Make a Whole				
24. Five Pieces Make a Whole				
25. Six Pieces Make a Whole				
26. Seven Pieces Make a Whole				
27. Eight Pieces Make a Whole				
28. Nine Pieces Make a Whole				
29. Ten Pieces Make a Whole				
SEQUENCE—TRACE OR DRAW, CUT, AND ASSEMBLE				
30. Above and Below				
31. Beginning, Middle, and End				
32. Big and Little				
33. First, Second, and Third				
34. In Front Of and Next to				
35. Layered				
36. Left and Right				
37. On and Off				
38. Young and Old				
LETTERS—TRACE OR WRITE, CUT, AND ASSEMBLE				
39. Letter of the Week				
40. First Letter of First Name				
41. First Letter of Last Name				
42. Letters We Love				
43. Sticks and Circles Letters				
44. Letter Outlines				

(continues)

THREE-STEP TRAY TASK	GOOD JOB	WITH HELP	NOT YET	COMMENTS
NUMBERS—TRACE, CUT, AND ASSEMBLE				
45. Number One and One Shape				
46. Number Two and Two Shapes				
47. Number Three and Three Shapes				
48. Number Four and Four Shapes				
49. Number Five and Five Shapes				
50. Number Six and Six Shapes				
51. Number Seven and Seven Shapes				
52. Number Eight and Eight Shapes				
53. Number Nine and Nine Shapes				
54. Number Ten and Ten Shapes				
TRACE OR RUB USING CHALK, FOLD, CUT, AND GLUE				
55. Fold, Cut, and Glue				
56. Multi-Fold, Cut, and Glue				
57. Rub, Cut, and Glue				
58. Trace, Cut, and Glue				
59. Parts Trace, Cut, and Glue				
60. Inset Reverse, Cut, and Glue				
USING RULER, DRAW, CUT, AND GLUE				
61. Large Square—Draw, Cut, and Glue				
62. Small Square—Draw, Cut, and Glue				
63. Large Rectangle—Draw, Cut, and Glue				
64. Small Rectangle—Draw, Cut, and Glue				
65. Large Triangle—Draw, Cut, and Glue				
66. Small Triangle—Draw, Cut, and Glue				
67. Large Diamond—Draw, Cut, and Glue				
68. Small Diamond—Draw, Cut, and Glue				
69. Large Pentagon—Draw, Cut, and Glue				

(continues)

THREE-STEP TRAY TASK	GOOD JOB	WITH HELP	NOT YET	COMMENTS
70. Small Pentagon—Draw, Cut, and Glue				
71. Multi Lines, Cut, and Glue				
72. Length Seriating, Cut, and Glue				
73. Height Seriating, Cut, and Glue				
74. Left-to-Right Lines, Cut, and Glue				
ORGANIZING AND ASSEMBLING BOOKLETS				
75. Alphabet Booklet				
76. Number Booklet				
77. Parts-to-a-Whole Booklet				
78. Sequencing Booklet				
79. Shape Booklet				
80. Size Booklet				

PORTFOLIO DOCUMENTATION

A portfolio contains a collection of children's work and the teacher's observations throughout the school year that informs families of children's progress through cognitive, physical, emotional, and social development. The most important information we share with families is the "growth over time" accomplishments from the school year. Create a portfolio by simply using a manila file folder or a binder for each child in your classroom.

Always date everything that you place in the folder so that you can chronologically display contents to show how a child is progressing throughout the year. Share the child's folder at conferences, when the child is moving to the next classroom, or upon completion of a school year.

The individual and classroom charts that are included in this section provide an ongoing method for teachers to observe and record each child's organizational skills progress and include evidence of learning in a portfolio that is shared with families throughout the school year. Keeping samples of tray tasks provides a valuable addition to other portfolio entry items to present a well-rounded picture of a child's abilities and progress throughout the school year.

Using a Portfolio as a Communication Tool

Include information about Three-Step Tray Tasks as part of your communication responsibilities to families as a means to explain how children are achieving essential skills for future learning.

Ways to communicate how learning is occurring in your program:

- Invite families to view a Three-Step Tray Task
- Have a child demonstrate a Three-Step Tray Task to families
- Copy and laminate an instruction page and display
- Demonstrate Three-Step Tray Tasks at open houses, meetings, and conferences
- Feature a Three-Step Tray Task in the front reception area
- Send home a Three-Step Tray Task family note throughout the school year so that families are informed of the method's importance. An example of a family note is included in this chapter.

By using an Individual Child Three-Step Tray Tasking Observation Chart you create a tool for documenting each child's organizational thinking skills. Authentic assessment is achieved by observing a child completing various Three-Step Tray Tasks. The chart becomes a part of your documentation process for program and family communication and validation of learning.

Make a copy for each child's portfolio. Fill in each child's name and age. It is recommended that you insert the date you observed the task being completed in the appropriate column of each child's chart.

Tasks need not be introduced in the order of the chart. The chart numbering reflects the task number in the book for convenience of locating each task.

⁂ SAMPLE LETTER TO FAMILIES ABOUT THREE-STEP TRAY TASKING

The following is a sample letter you may copy onto your school letterhead and distribute to families about the weekly tasks you are using. Informing families of children's progress is essential. *Three-Step Tray Tasking* offers authentic assessment tasks to verify that learning is happening in your classroom.

Date: _____

Dear Family of _____:

Your child is developing organizational thinking skills when completing a Three-Step Tray Task. This week we are emphasizing a Three-Step Tray Task called:

_____.

All Three-Step Tray Tasks are organized so that your child will experience the sequencing of beginning, middle, and end tasks that result in a finished project. By moving from left to right while performing each step of the task, your child is learning to process critical thinking skills and logical conclusions by:

✔ Using the whole body through purposeful actions

✔ Focusing the eyes and hands to work together to complete each task

✔ Crossing the midline of the body to promote left-to-right eye tracking for future reading

✔ Strengthening arm, wrist, and finger muscles by holding a pencil, chalk, markers, and scissors

We are observing your child's abilities and development using these skills building tasks.

Your child's teacher: _____

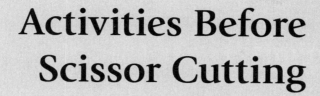

Chapter 2

Activities Before Scissor Cutting

FINE MOTOR DEVELOPMENT

Before you offer scissors to young children, the ability to tear needs to be introduced. Tearing paper is a multi-step movement. Using both hands and holding a piece of paper, children must move fingers and thumbs in the opposite direction at the same time in order to accomplish the tearing process. Tearing increases the arm, wrist, hand, and the finger muscles' pincer ability to work in concert with both hands simultaneously. Tearing one-inch strips of construction paper is a recommended beginning tearing activity. The tearing pieces may be placed in a collage box and transferred to the art area. Many opportunities for tearing different thicknesses of paper should occur before scissors are placed in a child's hand.

Paper plates, construction paper shapes, and recycled manila folders cut into shapes are good materials to provide children who are beginning to use scissors and are fringing or snipping. These activities should be available on a daily basis in the art area so children increase their abilities in fine muscle refinement, pincer control, and eye/hand coordination.

Teachers and adults may also offer children the opportunity to roll play dough into snakes to be used for cutting. Begin by offering children craft sticks or plastic knives for cutting the dough. Then, scissors may be used to cut the play dough snakes as a practice exercise before being offered paper to cut.

SCISSOR-CUTTING DEVELOPMENT

Scissor cutting provides teachers with a tangible way to observe and identify fine motor skills which are essential to coordinate the small muscles' ability to cut, grasp, and write. Successful scissor cutting heightens a child's ability to increase visual perception and develop eye/hand coordination skills. The hand coordination and eye perception must work together so that the cutting occurs where the eye signals the hand muscles to cut.

Current assessment evaluations as well as entrance or admissions tests in many school systems include scissor cutting as part of the screening process to measure a child's strengths and weaknesses of emerging skills.

Scissor cutting progresses through phases. The chart in this chapter emphasizes the basic steps toward successful scissor-cutting ability.

SCISSOR AND PENCIL HOLDING

Handedness may be determined by observing which hand a child picks up a pair of scissors or holds a pencil. Several tips are offered regarding the selection of scissors to insure that a child uses them safely and carefully. When choosing scissors, look for blunt tips and coated handles. Although many programs provide lefty scissors, safety scissors for young children may be used by both handedness. The chart in this chapter emphasizes safety rules when using scissors.

Picking up a pair of safety scissors provides a teacher with an indication of a child's handedness. Whichever hand the child manipulates the scissors

may well become the child's writing hand. Let's look at the components of holding scissors as shared in *Scissor Sorcery* by Sharan Bryant Carpenter (Humanics Limited, 1985).

1. **Position of the hand:** The fingers should be in correct relationship to the scissors.
2. **Grip strength in the hand:** The index finger and thumb should exhibit sufficient strength so that the scissor blades are forced to open and close.
3. **Angle at which the scissors are held:** The scissors should be in correct relationship to the material that is being cut.

Whenever observing a child picking up scissors, remind him or her to keep the "thumb up!" The thumb should be at the top so that the wrist is not turned or twisted. The tendency for children is to double their fingers through the holes in an attempt to grasp the handles. Correct finger placement is practiced with many of the *Three-Step Tray Tasking* activities.

Often children grasp pencils in the same fashion, doubling fingers around a pencil in order to gain control. The activities in this book will help strengthen small finger muscles which result in an increased ability to direct the pencil using a thumb and two-finger spread grasp. Rather than correct a

BEGINNING SCISSOR-CUTTING PHASES

Snipping (One snip motion)	Ability to precisely snip through narrow strips of paper or snip corners off of paper
Fringing (Multiple one snip motions)	Ability to cut with one snip multiple times around the edge of a piece of construction paper as if to fringe a place mat
Striping (Moving scissors across a short length of paper)	Ability to use the full length of the scissor blade and cut across a length of paper while the other hand holds the paper
Continuous Straight Line Cutting (Keeping scissor blade in the paper and moving across paper)	Ability to hold paper with one hand and hold scissors with the other hand and coordinate movements so that scissors move across a designated line or direction
Continuous Curved Line Cutting (Keeping scissor blade in paper and moving around paper)	Ability to move paper with one hand and hold scissors with the other hand and coordinate movements so that scissors move around a designated shape or curved line while other hand continuously moves the paper

child's grip choice, model the correct position each time you handle a pencil or other writing tools. Children should learn to hold and manipulate pencils and scissors correctly until they feel comfortable and able to proceed.

Eye/hand coordination is an essential skill and is exercised with every activity. Eye/hand coordination is how the hands and body and other muscles respond to the information gathered through the eyes. Without opportunities to refine eye and hand movement, children may find it difficult to advance toward writing and reading skill success. The tasks promote the crossing of the midline which is an imaginary vertical line running down the middle of the body. When we cross over the midline with arms or legs, we are integrating both sides of the body to work in harmony. The midline also serves as a crossover for the eyes when tracking or following objects or symbols. This ability leads toward the acquisition of reading and writing skills through the refinement of the coordination of eye and hand movements.

STORING SCISSORS

Whenever children are using scissors, care must be used so that accidents do not occur. Rules for scissor care should become part of the classroom expectations. A suggested list of safety rules can be found at the end of this chapter.

Suggestions for ways to store individual or sets of scissors:

- Covered small frozen juice cans
- Upside-down egg cartons
- Several stacked upside-down Styrofoam vegetable trays
- Large piece of packing foam placed in a shoe box lid
- Play dough packed inside half of an empty toilet paper tube
- Commercial scissor rack

USE OF STENCILS

Tasks call for the use of stencils. The stencil templates are located on the Online Companion Web site at www.earlychilded.delmar.com. Teachers can print, copy, and cut the paper stencils and create cardboard or poster board versions to be used with the tasks. Younger children are more successful in tracing inside a stencil rather than tracing around the outside edge of a stencil. Determine the ability of your children by providing stencils in the art area, and observe how well children handle the different types when attempting to trace. Substitute one type for another when setting up a tray task and document each child's ability. You can promote children from the stencil to a template throughout the school year.

CLASSROOM SCISSOR SAFETY RULES

1. Scissors are only used for cutting activities.

2. We always keep scissors at a particular location and never walk or run with scissors in hand.

3. Scissors can hurt so attention to scissor handling is a must.

4. When handing scissors to a friend, hold the handle up and point the end down toward the ground.

5. Store scissors in appropriate containers only.

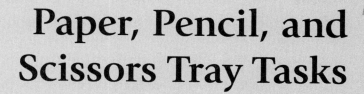

Chapter 3

Paper, Pencil, and Scissors Tray Tasks

The following tasks require paper, a stencil, a pencil or colored pencil, scissors, and a glue stick. By using these tools, children engage in purposeful manipulation of classroom materials in an organized method. Most teachers think of paper, pencils, glue, and scissors as part of the art or writing areas of the classroom. This book creates a new organizational method using familiar tools. All task materials should be kept separate from similar materials in other parts of the classroom. They are chosen to be used in specific ways with each tray. The arrangement of the materials focuses a child's ability to construct a task following a specific sequence. Tasks build concentration, problem solving, and attention to detail. Teachers may choose the tasks in this section in the order followed by the book, or select a task based on current individual needs.

SECTION I—SHAPE—TRACE, CUT, AND ASSEMBLE

Task 1

Circle Shape

This section offers children the opportunity to explore shapes by using shape stencils as well as practice in cutting and gluing. The tasks emphasize circle, oval, crescent, square, rectangle, triangle, diamond, pentagon, hexagon, and octagon shapes.

 Print the stencil templates found on the Online Companion located at www.earlychilded.delmar.com and make each shape on poster or cardboard, purchase store-bought shape stencils, or create teacher-made shapes of your own.

The different shapes for these tasks help children identify common shapes. Select a tray task based on your current theme or emphasis, such as using the octagon shape when discussing stop signs. Ask children to identify objects in the room that match the shape they are tracing, cutting, and gluing.

Materials:

- Three plastic rectangular trays
- White paper to fit the tray
- A primary pencil
- Circle stencil
- Scissors
- Construction paper to fit the tray
- Glue stick

Setup:

1. Place three trays in a horizontal row
2. **1st Tray:** Place white paper and pencil on tray
3. **2nd Tray:** Place scissors either in an individual holder or across the top of the tray
4. **3rd Tray:** Place colored paper on tray with a glue stick at the top of the tray

1st Tray

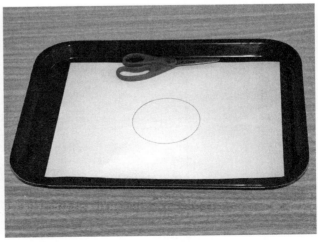

2nd Tray

Some of the task pictures show a container to hold stencils, pencils, and markers. Other tasks do not show a container. You may choose to use a container or not. It depends on the available space to set up the tasks. Some of the task pictures show the pencil or other tracing instrument at the top of the tray or on the left side of the tray. Either position is appropriate as we are emphasizing both top-to-bottom and left-to-right directions.

Many of the pictures show a stencil that is solid in the middle and the child traces around the shape. Others will show a cut-out stencil for the child to trace inside the frame to create a shape. Both of these types of stencils are appropriate to use. The pictures vary the options for presentation ideas.

Task:

1. **Beginning:** The goal is for the child to use the pencil and trace the shape.
2. **Middle:** The goal is to transfer the traced shape to the second tray and use the scissors to cut out the drawn shape.
3. **End:** The goal is to transfer the cut circle to the third tray and glue onto a contrasting color of paper.

Outcome:

By completing this task a child learns that a circle shape has no corners. A child learns to follow directions, manipulate materials, and complete a task. Teachers have the opportunity to discuss the name and attributes of the shape.

Emerging Skills:

This task helps children to strengthen their eye/hand coordination and increase dexterity in pencil and scissor skills.

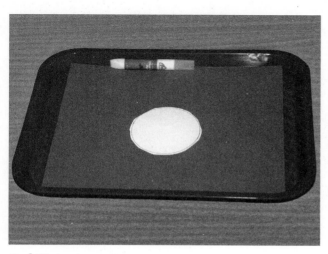

3rd Tray

Task 2

Oval Shape

⦚⦚⦚ Materials:

- Three plastic rectangular trays
- White paper to fit the tray
- A primary pencil
- Oval stencil
- Scissors
- Construction paper to fit the tray
- Glue stick

⦚⦚⦚ Setup:

1. Place three trays in a horizontal row
2. **1st Tray:** Place white paper and pencil on tray
3. **2nd Tray:** Place scissors either in an individual holder or across the top of the tray
4. **3rd Tray:** Place colored paper on tray with a glue stick at the top of the tray

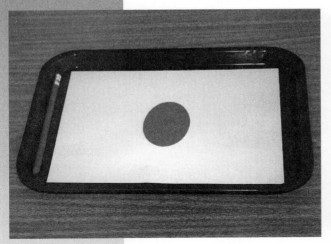

1st Tray

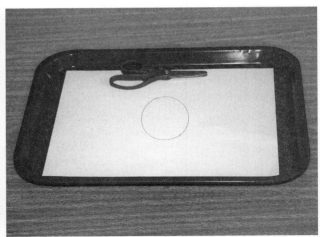

2nd Tray

Task:

1. **Beginning:** The goal is for the child to use the pencil and trace the shape.
2. **Middle:** The goal is to transfer the traced shape to the second tray and use the scissors to cut out.
3. **End:** The goal is to transfer the cut oval shape to the third tray and glue onto a contrasting color of paper.

 ### Outcome:

By completing this task a child learns about round shapes other than circles and that this shape is called an oval. A child learns to follow directions, manipulate materials, and complete a task. Teachers have the opportunity to discuss the name and attributes of the shape by comparing the oval to a circle.

 ### Emerging Skills:

This task helps children to strengthen their eye/hand coordination and increase dexterity in pencil and scissor skills. The child is also expanding his or her vocabulary by learning the name of the shape and applying that knowledge to other objects in the classroom.

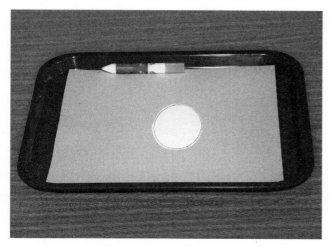

3rd Tray

Task 3

Crescent Shape

Materials:

- Three plastic rectangular trays
- White paper to fit the tray
- A primary pencil
- Crescent stencil
- Scissors
- Construction paper to fit the tray
- Glue stick

Setup:

1. Place three trays in a horizontal row
2. **1st Tray:** Place white paper and pencil on tray
3. **2nd Tray:** Place scissors either in an individual holder or across the top of the tray
4. **3rd Tray:** Place colored paper on tray with a glue stick at the top of the tray

1st Tray

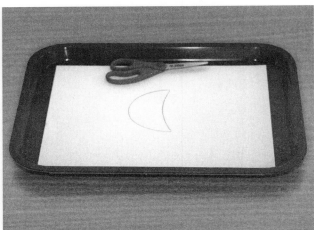

2nd Tray

Task:

1. **Beginning:** The goal is for the child to use the pencil and trace the shape.
2. **Middle:** The goal is to transfer the traced shape to the second tray and use the scissors to cut out.
3. **End:** The goal is to transfer the cut crescent shape to the third tray and glue onto a contrasting color of paper.

Outcome:

By completing this task a child learns about a shape called a crescent. A child learns to follow directions, manipulate materials, and complete a task. Teachers have the opportunity to discuss the name and attributes of the shape by comparing the crescent shape to a phase of the Moon.

Emerging Skills:

This task helps children to strengthen their eye/hand coordination and increase dexterity in pencil and scissor skills. The child is also expanding his or her vocabulary by learning the name of the shape and applying that knowledge when speaking about the objects that are crescent-shaped such as a banana or a boomerang.

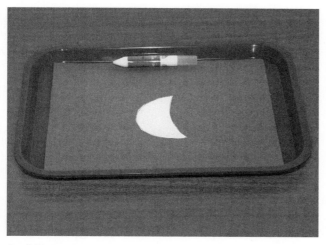

3rd Tray

Task 4

Square Shape

))) *Materials:*

- Three plastic rectangular trays
- White paper to fit the tray
- A primary pencil
- Square stencil
- Scissors
- Construction paper to fit the tray
- Glue stick

))) *Setup:*

1. Place three trays in a horizontal row
2. **1st Tray:** Place white paper and pencil on tray
3. **2nd Tray:** Place scissors either in an individual holder or across the top of the tray
4. **3rd Tray:** Place colored paper on tray with a glue stick at the top of the tray

1st Tray

2nd Tray

Task:

1. **Beginning:** The goal is for the child to use the pencil and trace the shape.
2. **Middle:** The goal is to transfer the traced shape to the second tray and use the scissors to cut out.
3. **End:** The goal is to transfer the cut square shape to the third tray and glue onto a contrasting color of paper.

 Outcome:

By completing this task a child learns about a shape that has four corners called a square. A child learns to follow directions, manipulate materials, and complete a task.

Emerging Skills:

This task helps children to strengthen their eye/hand coordination and increase dexterity in pencil and scissor skills. The child is also expanding his or her vocabulary by learning the name of the shape and applying that knowledge to other objects in the classroom.

3rd Tray

Task 5

Rectangle Shape

))) Materials:

- Three plastic rectangular trays
- White paper to fit the tray
- A primary pencil
- Rectangle stencil
- Scissors
- Construction paper to fit the tray
- Glue stick

))) Setup:

1. Place three trays in a horizontal row
2. **1st Tray:** Place white paper and pencil on tray
3. **2nd Tray:** Place scissors either in an individual holder or across the top of the tray
4. **3rd Tray:** Place colored paper on tray with a glue stick at the top of the tray

1st Tray

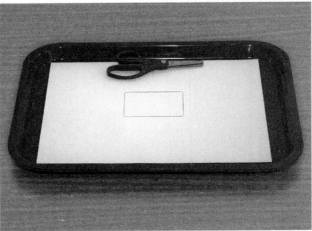

2nd Tray

 ## Task:

1. **Beginning:** The goal is for the child to use the pencil and trace the shape.
2. **Middle:** The goal is to transfer the traced shape to the second tray and use the scissors to cut out.
3. **End:** The goal is to transfer the cut rectangle shape to the third tray and glue onto a contrasting color of paper.

Outcome:

By completing this task a child learns about a shape that has corners other than a square. A child learns to follow directions, manipulate materials, and complete a task. Teachers have the opportunity to discuss the name and attributes of the shape by comparing the rectangle to a square.

Emerging Skills:

This task helps children to strengthen their eye/hand coordination and increase dexterity in pencil and scissor skills. The child is also expanding his or her vocabulary by learning the name of the shape, comparing objects such as the wooden or plastic blocks in the classroom, and sorting the squares and the rectangles.

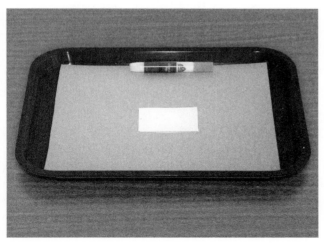

3rd Tray

Task 6

Triangle Shape

⚒ Materials:

- Three plastic rectangular trays
- White paper to fit the tray
- A primary pencil
- Triangle stencil
- Scissors
- Construction paper to fit the tray
- Glue stick

⚒ Setup:

1. Place three trays in a horizontal row
2. **1st Tray:** Place white paper and pencil on tray
3. **2nd Tray:** Place scissors either in an individual holder or across the top of the tray
4. **3rd Tray:** Place colored paper on tray with a glue stick at the top of the tray

1st Tray

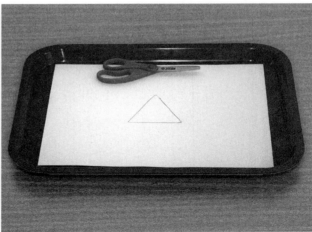

2nd Tray

Task:

1. **Beginning:** The goal is for the child to use the pencil and trace the shape.
2. **Middle:** The goal is to transfer the traced shape to the second tray and use the scissors to cut out.
3. **End:** The goal is to transfer the cut triangle shape to the third tray and glue onto a contrasting color of paper.

Outcome:

By completing this task a child learns about a shape that has corners other than a square. A child learns to follow directions, manipulate materials, and complete a task. Teachers have the opportunity to discuss the name and attributes of the shape by comparing the triangle to the rectangle and the square. The child discovers that a triangle has only three corners.

Emerging Skills:

This task helps children to strengthen their eye/hand coordination and increase dexterity in pencil and scissor skills. The child is also expanding his or her vocabulary by learning the name of the shape, comparing objects such as the wooden or plastic blocks in the classroom, and sorting the triangles, squares, and rectangles into like groups.

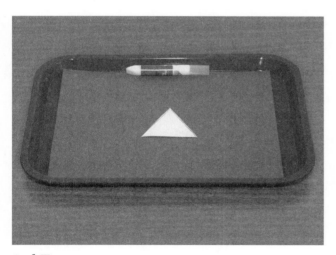

3rd Tray

Task 7

Diamond Shape

))) Materials:

- Three plastic rectangular trays
- White paper to fit the tray
- A primary pencil
- Diamond stencil
- Scissors
- Construction paper to fit the tray
- Glue stick

))) Setup:

1. Place three trays in a horizontal row
2. **1st Tray:** Place white paper and pencil on tray
3. **2nd Tray:** Place scissors either in an individual holder or across the top of the tray
4. **3rd Tray:** Place colored paper on tray with a glue stick at the top of the tray

1st Tray

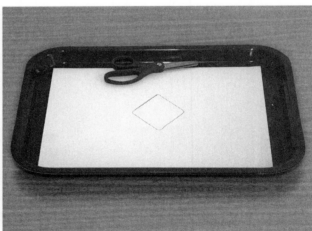

2nd Tray

⁞⁞⁞ Task:

1. **Beginning:** The goal is for the child to use the pencil to trace the shape.
2. **Middle:** The goal is to transfer the traced shape to the second tray and use the scissors to cut out.
3. **End:** The goal is to transfer the cut diamond shape to the third tray and glue onto a contrasting color of paper.

⁞⁞⁞ Outcome:

By completing this task a child learns to follow directions, manipulate materials, and complete a task. Teachers have the opportunity to discuss the name and attributes of the shape by comparing the diamond to a rectangle and a square.

⁞⁞⁞ Emerging Skills:

This task helps children to strengthen their eye/hand coordination and increase dexterity in pencil and scissor skills. The child is also expanding his or her vocabulary by learning the name of the shape and comparing objects by turning wooden or plastic squares into diamonds. Teachers may challenge a child to create a repeating pattern with blocks making a square, diamond, square, or diamond pattern on the floor. Then ask the child to tell you the name of each block shape starting at the beginning of the row and moving left to right.

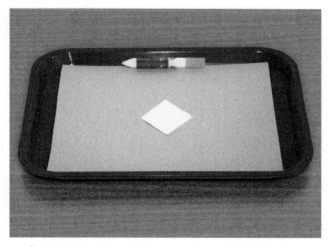

3rd Tray

Task 8

Pentagon Shape

⧼ Materials:

- Three plastic rectangular trays
- White paper to fit the tray
- A primary pencil
- Pentagon stencil
- Scissors
- Construction paper to fit the tray
- Glue stick

⧼ Setup:

1. Place three trays in a horizontal row
2. **1st Tray:** Place white paper and pencil on tray
3. **2nd Tray:** Place scissors either in an individual holder or across the top of the tray
4. **3rd Tray:** Place colored paper on tray with a glue stick at the top of the tray

1st Tray

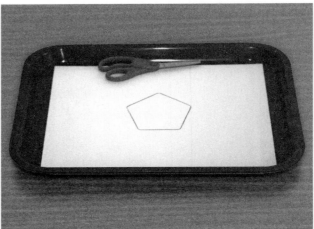

2nd Tray

Task:

1. **Beginning:** The goal is for the child to use the pencil and trace the shape.
2. **Middle:** The goal is to transfer the traced shape to the second tray and use the scissors to cut out.
3. **End:** The goal is to transfer the cut pentagon shape to the third tray and glue onto a contrasting color of paper.

Outcome:

By completing this task a child learns about a shape that has five corners called a pentagon. A child learns to follow directions, manipulate materials, and complete a task. Teachers have the opportunity to discuss the name and attributes of the shape and compare a pentagon to a drawing of the outline of a house.

Emerging Skills:

This task helps children to strengthen their eye/hand coordination and increase dexterity in pencil and scissor skills. This shape may be compared to the shape of home plate in baseball or a picture of the U.S. Department of Defense building in Washington DC called the Pentagon.

3rd Tray

Task 9

Hexagon Shape

Materials:

- Three plastic rectangular trays
- White paper to fit the tray
- A primary pencil
- Hexagon stencil
- Scissors
- Construction paper to fit the tray
- Glue stick

Setup:

1. Place three trays in a horizontal row
2. **1st Tray:** Place white paper and pencil on tray
3. **2nd Tray:** Place scissors either in an individual holder or across the top of the tray
4. **3rd Tray:** Place colored paper on tray with a glue stick at the top of the tray

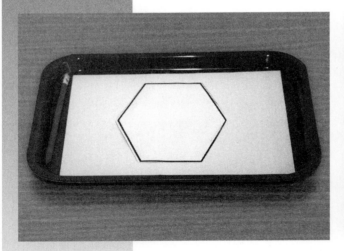

1st Tray

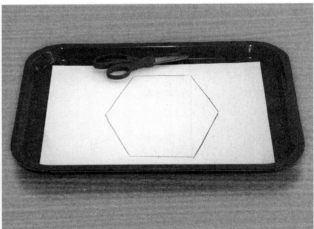

2nd Tray

Task:

1. **Beginning:** The goal is for the child to use the pencil and trace the shape.
2. **Middle:** The goal is to transfer the traced hexagon shape to the second tray and use the scissors to cut out.
3. **End:** The goal is to transfer the cut hexagon shape to the third tray and glue onto a contrasting color of paper.

Outcome:

By completing this task a child learns about a shape that has six sides and six corners called a hexagon. A child learns to follow directions, manipulate materials, and complete a task.

Emerging Skills:

This task helps children to strengthen their eye/hand coordination and increase dexterity in pencil and scissor skills. The child is also expanding his or her vocabulary by learning the name of the shape and thinking about objects that may resemble that shape.

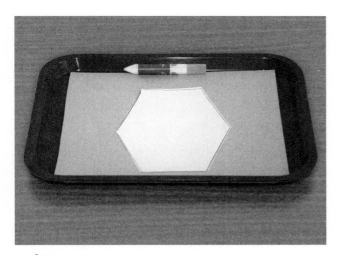

3rd Tray

Task 10

Octagon Shape

⟩⟩⟩ Materials:

- Three plastic rectangular trays
- White paper to fit the tray
- A primary pencil
- Octagon stencil
- Scissors
- Construction paper to fit the tray
- Glue stick

⟩⟩⟩ Setup:

1. Place three trays in a horizontal row
2. **1st Tray:** Place white paper and pencil on tray
3. **2nd Tray:** Place scissors either in an individual holder or across the top of the tray
4. **3rd Tray:** Place colored paper on tray with a glue stick at the top of the tray

1st Tray

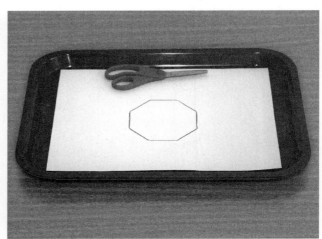

2nd Tray

Task:

1. **Beginning:** The goal is for the child to use the pencil and trace the shape.
2. **Middle:** The goal is to transfer the traced shape to the second tray and use the scissors to cut out.
3. **End:** The goal is to transfer the cut octagon shape to the third tray and glue onto a contrasting color of paper.

Outcome:

By completing this task a child learns about a shape that has eight sides and eight corners called an octagon. A child learns to follow directions, manipulate materials, and complete a task. Teachers have the opportunity to discuss the name and attributes of the shape.

Emerging Skills:

This task helps children to strengthen their eye/hand coordination and increase dexterity in pencil and scissor skills. The child is also expanding his or her vocabulary by learning the name of the shape and comparing it to a common traffic sign—the stop sign.

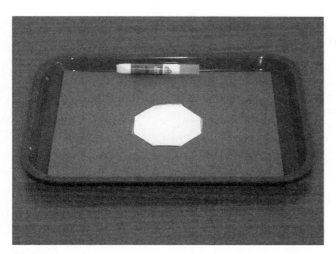

3rd Tray

SECTION II—SIZE—TRACE OR DRAW, CUT, AND ASSEMBLE

Task 11

Small, Medium, and Large Circles

This section offers several ways to incorporate the concept of size in a three-step tray task. The tasks emphasize circle, oval, crescent, square, rectangle, triangle, diamond, pentagon, hexagon, and octagon shapes in small, medium, and large sizes.

 Print the stencil templates found on the Online Companion located at www.earlychilded.delmar.com and make each shape on poster or cardboard, purchase store-bought shape stencils, or create teacher-made shapes of your own.

Materials:

- Three plastic rectangular trays
- White paper to fit tray
- Colored pencils
- Three sizes of circle-shape stencils
- Scissors
- Construction paper to fit tray
- Glue stick

Setup:

1. Place three trays in a horizontal row
2. Place colored pencils in a container to the left of the tray
3. **1st Tray:** Place white paper and circle stencils on tray
4. **2nd Tray:** Place scissors either in an individual holder or across the top of the tray
5. **3rd Tray:** Place sheet of colored paper with glue stick at top of tray

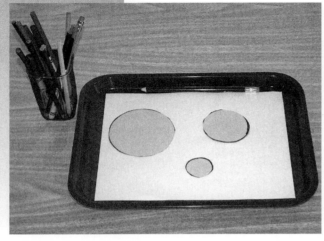

1st Tray

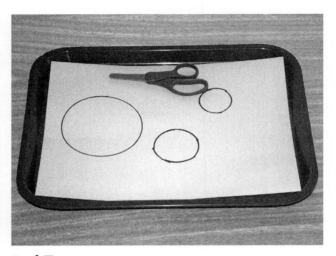

2nd Tray

Task:

1. **Beginning:** The goal is for the child to trace three sizes of a circle on the paper.
2. **Middle:** The goal is for the child to transfer the paper with traced shapes and use the scissors to cut out three circles.
3. **End:** The goal is for the child to transfer the cut shapes gluing onto the colored construction paper in a small, medium, and large sequence.

Outcome:

By completing this task a child learns to practice size identification and discrimination by identifying the small, medium, and large shapes. The child demonstrates his or her knowledge of sizing by sequencing the shapes onto the paper in a small, medium, and large order.

Emerging Skills:

This task helps children process several movements at the same time during tracing, cutting, and gluing. The child will also practice crossing the midline while tracing, cutting, and gluing.

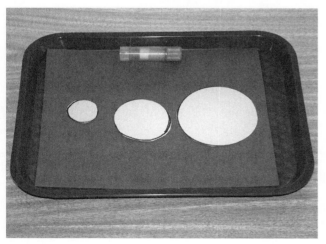

3rd Tray

Task 12

Small, Medium, and Large Ovals

⧊ *Materials:*

- Three plastic rectangular trays
- White paper to fit tray
- Colored pencil
- Three sizes of oval-shape stencils
- Scissors
- Construction paper to fit tray
- Glue stick

⧊ *Setup:*

1. Place three trays in a horizontal row
2. **1st Tray:** Place white paper, colored pencil, and shape stencils on tray
3. **2nd Tray:** Place scissors either in an individual holder or across the top of the tray
4. **3rd Tray:** Place sheet of colored paper on tray with glue stick at top of tray

1st Tray

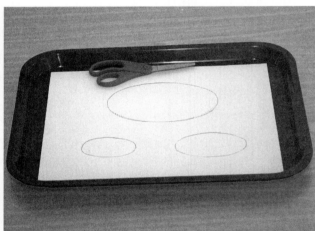

2nd Tray

Task:

1. **Beginning:** The goal is for the child to place three different sizes of an oval on white paper and trace around each shape.
2. **Middle:** The goal is for the child to transfer the traced shapes to the 2nd tray and cut out shapes with scissors.
3. **End:** The goal is for the child to glue shapes in a small, medium, and large sequence on colored paper.

Outcome:

By completing this task a child learns to practice size identification and discrimination by identifying the small, medium, and large ovals. The child demonstrates his or her knowledge of sizing by sequencing the ovals onto the paper in a small, medium, and large order. The child also thinks about the best way to organize the shapes on the paper to achieve the correct sizing sequence.

Emerging Skills:

This task helps children discriminate sizes and practice crossing the midline while tracing, cutting, and gluing.

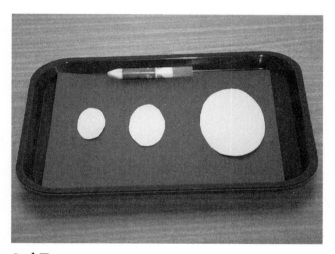

3rd Tray

Task 13

Small, Medium, and Large Crescents

〰 *Materials:*

- Three plastic rectangular trays
- White paper to fit tray
- Colored pencil
- Three sizes of crescent-shape stencils
- Scissors
- Construction paper to fit tray
- Glue stick

〰 *Setup:*

1. Place three trays in a horizontal row
2. **1st Tray:** Place white paper, colored pencil, and three different sizes of crescent shapes on tray
3. **2nd Tray:** Place scissors either in an individual holder or across the top of the tray
4. **3rd Tray:** Place sheet of colored paper on tray with glue stick at top of tray

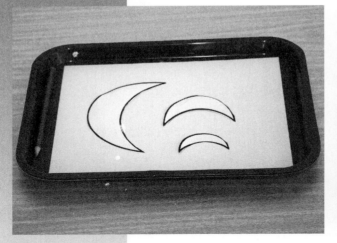

1st Tray

2nd Tray

Task:

1. **Beginning:** The goal is for the child to use a colored pencil and trace three crescent shapes in small, medium, and large sizes.
2. **Middle:** The goal is for the child to transfer the paper to the second tray and use the scissors to cut the three shape sizes.
3. **End:** The goal is for the child to transfer the shapes and glue the three cut shapes in a small, medium, and large sequence.

 ## Outcome:

By completing this task a child creates shapes in three sizes. The child demonstrates discrimination of sizing by sequencing the crescents onto the paper in a small, medium, and large order. The child also thinks about the best way to organize the shapes on the paper to achieve the correct sizing sequence.

Emerging Skills:

This task helps children assign a name to the shape and a size attribute when identifying each shape.

3rd Tray

Task 14

Small, Medium, and Large Squares

⧼ Materials:

- Three plastic rectangular trays
- White paper to fit tray
- Colored pencil
- Three sizes of square-shape stencils
- Scissors
- Construction paper to fit tray
- Glue stick

⧼ Setup:

1. Place three trays in a horizontal row
2. **1st Tray:** Place white paper, colored pencil, and shapes on tray
3. **2nd Tray:** Place scissors either in an individual holder or across the top of the tray
4. **3rd Tray:** Place sheet of colored paper on tray with glue stick at top of tray

1st Tray

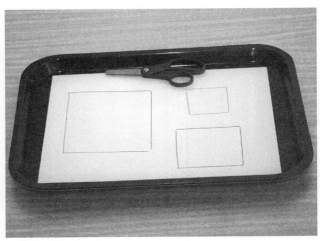

2nd Tray

ⅷⅷ *Task:*

1. **Beginning:** The goal is for the child to use a colored pencil and trace three sizes of square shapes.
2. **Middle:** The goal is for the child to transfer the paper to the second tray and use the scissors to cut the three shape sizes.
3. **End:** The goal is for the child to transfer the shapes and glue the three cut shapes in a small, medium, and large sequence.

ⅷⅷ *Outcome:*

By completing this task a child creates shapes in three sizes and discriminates the order of the sizes when gluing.

ⅷⅷ *Emerging Skills:*

The child problem solves how to place three shapes on one sheet of paper while refining eye/hand coordination when cutting, gluing, and assembling. Teachers may ask a child to find objects in the classroom that are small, medium, and large in size and sequence them on the floor or a table.

3rd Tray

Task 15

Small, Medium, and Large Rectangles

⁓ Materials:

- Three plastic rectangular trays
- White paper to fit tray
- Colored pencil
- Three sizes of rectangle-shape stencils
- Scissors
- Construction paper to fit tray
- Glue stick

⁓ Setup:

1. Place three trays in a horizontal row
2. **1st Tray:** Place white paper, colored pencil, and rectangle stencils on tray
3. **2nd Tray:** Place scissors either in an individual holder or across the top of the tray
4. **3rd Tray:** Place sheet of colored paper on tray with glue stick at top of tray

1st Tray

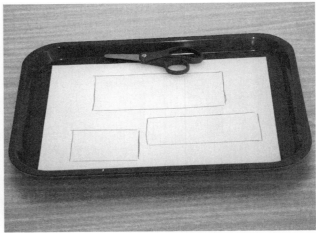

2nd Tray

Task:

1. **Beginning:** The goal is for the child to use a colored pencil and trace three sizes of rectangle shapes.
2. **Middle:** The goal is for the child to transfer the paper to the second tray and use the scissors to cut the three shape sizes.
3. **End:** The goal is for the child to transfer the shapes and glue the three cut shapes in a small, medium, and large sequence.

Outcome:

By completing this task a child creates rectangle shapes in three sizes and decides how to position the order of the sizes when gluing.

Emerging Skills:

The child practices problem-solving skills when organizing three shapes on one sheet of paper while refining eye/hand coordination when cutting, gluing, and assembling.

3rd Tray

Task 16

Small, Medium, and Large Triangles

))) Materials:

- Three plastic rectangular trays
- White paper to fit tray
- Colored pencil
- Three sizes of triangle-shape stencils
- Scissors
- Construction paper to fit tray
- Glue stick

))) Setup:

1. Place three trays in a horizontal row
2. **1st Tray:** Place white paper, colored pencil, and shapes on tray
3. **2nd Tray:** Place scissors either in an individual holder or across the top of the tray
4. **3rd Tray:** Place sheet of colored paper on tray with glue stick at top of tray

1st Tray

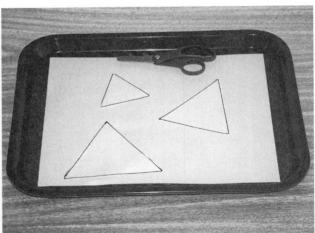

2nd Tray

Task:

1. **Beginning:** The goal is for the child to use a colored pencil and trace three triangle shapes in small, medium, and large sizes.
2. **Middle:** The goal is for the child to transfer the paper to the second tray and use the scissors to cut the three shape sizes.
3. **End:** The goal is for the child to transfer the shapes and glue the three cut shapes in a small, medium, and large sequence.

Outcome:

This task requires a child to cut three different sizes of the same shape and place on the assembling paper in a small, medium, and large order.

Emerging Skills:

The child develops problem-solving skills when deciding how to place three shapes on one sheet of paper while refining eye/hand coordination as he or she traces, cuts, and glues.

3rd Tray

Task 17

Small, Medium, and Large Diamonds

⧼ Materials:

- Three plastic rectangular trays
- White paper to fit tray
- Colored pencil
- Three sizes of diamond-shape stencils
- Scissors
- Construction paper to fit tray
- Glue stick

⧼ Setup:

1. Place three trays in a horizontal row
2. **1st Tray:** Place white paper, colored pencil, and shapes on tray
3. **2nd Tray:** Place scissors either in an individual holder or across the top of the tray
4. **3rd Tray:** Place sheet of colored paper on tray with glue stick at top of tray

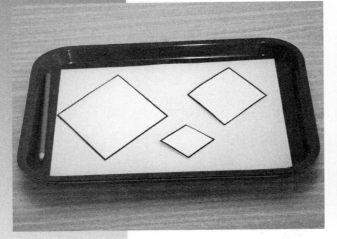

1st Tray

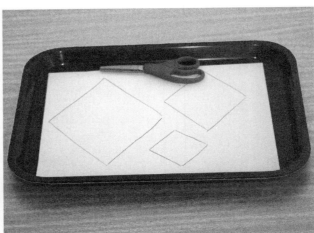

2nd Tray

Task:

1. **Beginning:** The goal is for the child to use a colored pencil and trace three diamond shapes in small, medium, and large sizes.
2. **Middle:** The goal is for the child to transfer the paper to the second tray and use the scissors to cut the three shape sizes.
3. **End:** The goal is for the child to transfer the shapes and glue the three cut diamond shapes in a small, medium, and large sequence.

 ## Outcome:

This task provides an opportunity for a child to trace, cut, and assemble a diamond shape in three sizes.

 ## Emerging Skills:

A child uses his or her problem-solving skills when placing three shapes on one sheet of paper. This task helps a child discriminate sizing attributes of a shape.

3rd Tray

Task 18

Small, Medium, and Large Pentagons

))) Materials:

- Three plastic rectangular trays
- White paper to fit tray
- Colored pencil
- Three sizes of pentagon-shape stencils
- Scissors
- Construction paper to fit tray
- Glue stick

))) Setup:

1. Place three trays in a horizontal row
2. **1st Tray:** Place white paper, colored pencil, and shapes on tray
3. **2nd Tray:** Place scissors either in an individual holder or across the top of the tray
4. **3rd Tray:** Place sheet of colored paper on tray with glue stick at top of tray

1st Tray

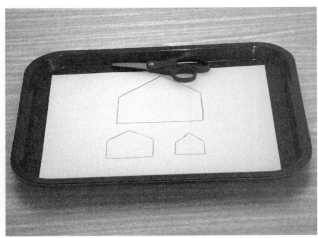

2nd Tray

Task:

1. **Beginning:** The goal is for the child to use a colored pencil and trace three pentagon shapes in small, medium, and large sizes.
2. **Middle:** The goal is for the child to transfer the paper to the second tray and use the scissors to cut the three shape sizes.
3. **End:** The goal is for the child to transfer the shapes and glue the three cut shapes in a small, medium, and large sequence.

Outcome:

The child creates pentagon shapes in three sizes and places them in a small, medium, and large order.

Emerging Skills:

The child utilizes problem-solving skills when deciding how to position three shapes on one sheet of paper while he or she strengthens eye/hand coordination when cutting, gluing, and assembling.

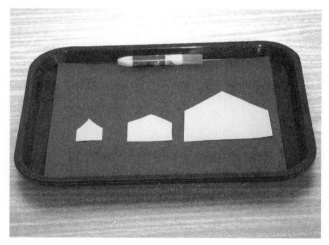

3rd Tray

Task 19

Small, Medium, and Large Hexagons

⟩⟩⟩ Materials:

- Three plastic rectangular trays
- White paper to fit tray
- Colored pencil
- Three sizes of hexagon-shape stencils
- Scissors
- Construction paper to fit tray
- Glue stick

⟩⟩⟩ Setup:

1. Place three trays in a horizontal row
2. **1st Tray:** Place white paper, colored pencil, and shapes on tray
3. **2nd Tray:** Place scissors either in an individual holder or across the top of the tray
4. **3rd Tray:** Place sheet of colored paper on tray with glue stick at top of tray

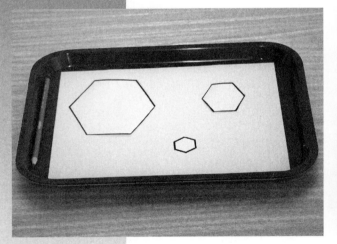

1st Tray

2nd Tray

))) Task:

1. **Beginning:** The goal is for the child to use a colored pencil and trace three hexagons in small, medium, and large sizes.
2. **Middle:** The goal is for the child to transfer the paper to the second tray and use the scissors to cut the three shape sizes.
3. **End:** The goal is for the child to transfer the shapes and glue the three cut shapes in a small, medium, and large sequence.

))) Outcome:

This task encourages a child to trace, cut, and glue shapes in three sizes. The child learns that hexagons may be sequenced in a small, medium, and large order.

))) Emerging Skills:

While sequencing the order of the hexagons, the child problem solves as to how to place three shapes on one sheet of paper in the correct order. While assembling, the child is organizing his or her thoughts about what came first, next, and last in this three-step process.

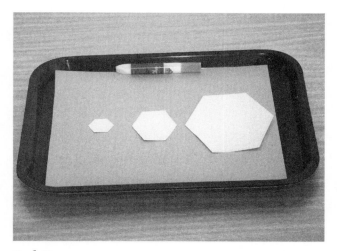

3rd Tray

Task 20

Small, Medium, and Large Octagons

Materials:

- Three plastic rectangular trays
- White paper to fit tray
- Colored pencil
- Three sizes of octagon-shape stencils
- Scissors
- Construction paper to fit tray
- Glue stick

Setup:

1. Place three trays in a horizontal row
2. **1st Tray:** Place white paper, colored pencil, and shapes on tray
3. **2nd Tray:** Place scissors either in an individual holder or across the top of the tray
4. **3rd Tray:** Place sheet of colored paper on tray with glue stick at top of tray

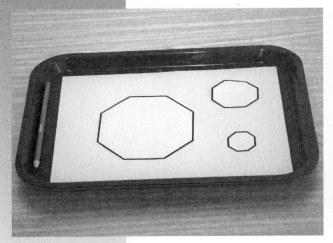

1st Tray

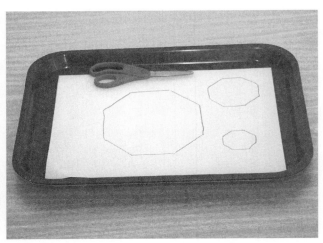

2nd Tray

Task:

1. **Beginning:** The goal is for the child to use a colored pencil and trace three octagon shapes in small, medium, and large sizes.
2. **Middle:** The goal is for the child to transfer the paper to the second tray and use the scissors to cut the three shape sizes.
3. **End:** The goal is for the child to transfer and glue the three cut shapes in a small, medium, and large sequence.

Outcome:

As a child creates shapes in three sizes, he or she discriminates the order of the sizes when gluing.

Emerging Skills:

This task helps children learn to problem solve how to place three shapes on one sheet of paper. The child also refines his or her eye/hand coordination when cutting, gluing, and assembling.

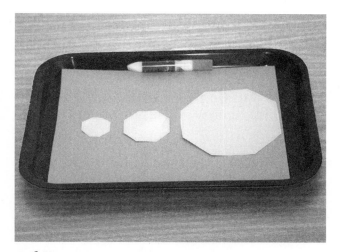

3rd Tray

SECTION III—PARTS TO A WHOLE— TRACE, CUT, AND ASSEMBLE

Task 21

Two Pieces Make a Whole

The following three-step tray tasks concentrate on the concept of parts to a whole. The purpose of the tasks is to provide children with the opportunity of cutting a whole shape into smaller pieces, then reassembling to become a whole again. The child may associate these tasks with putting a puzzle back together again.

This section may be used in conjunction with a concentrated focus in the classroom on the mathematical concepts of parts to a whole, fractions, or counting for pre-kindergarten and kindergarten programs. It is recommended that teachers create integrated learning exercises such as cooking and art experiences that reinforce these concepts.

Materials:

- Three plastic rectangular trays
- White paper to fit tray
- Colored pencil
- Triangle stencil
- Scissors
- Construction paper to fit tray
- Glue stick

Setup:

1. Place three trays in a horizontal row
2. **1st Tray:** Place white paper, triangle stencil, and a colored pencil on first tray
3. **2nd Tray:** Place scissors at the top of the tray
4. **3rd Tray:** Place colored paper on tray with glue stick at top of tray

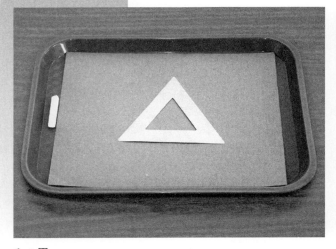

1st Tray

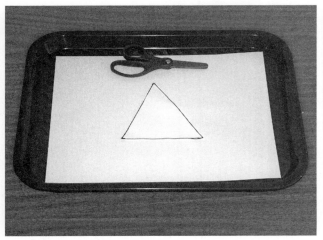

2nd Tray

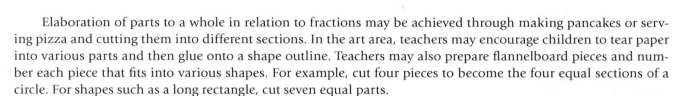

Elaboration of parts to a whole in relation to fractions may be achieved through making pancakes or serving pizza and cutting them into different sections. In the art area, teachers may encourage children to tear paper into various parts and then glue onto a shape outline. Teachers may also prepare flannelboard pieces and number each piece that fits into various shapes. For example, cut four pieces to become the four equal sections of a circle. For shapes such as a long rectangle, cut seven equal parts.

When cutting the shape into pieces, the child may attempt to cut parts in several suggested ways; free-hand cutting using a ruler to draw lines across the shape, or folding the shape and cutting on the folds. Children may investigate how to cut something into three pieces in nontraditional ways, such as cutting straight across the shape. They may also cut one piece in half, then cut the piece in half again. Teachers may suggest the various options and ways to achieve the goal of the task.

⅜ Task:

1. **Beginning:** The goal is for the child to trace the stencil onto white paper using a colored pencil.
2. **Middle:** The goal is to transfer paper to 2nd tray and cut out triangle. The child is to then cut the triangle in two pieces. (You may elect to draw a line down the middle of the shape for child to cut in half; the child may also draw a line or may elect to freely cut the shape in two pieces.)
3. **End:** The goal is to transfer two pieces and place on colored paper, gluing to form the whole shape again.

⅜ Outcome:

By completing this task a child learns that two pieces of a shape make a whole shape again when reassembled.

⅜ Emerging Skills:

The child begins to understand two parts equal a whole when assembling this task.

⅜ Extension Activity:

The following extension activity is for children who comprehend the meaning of math terms such as equal halves and symbol matching. A child would need to be able to cut the shape into two equal parts.

* Write each of the five symbols of the math problem ($\frac{1}{2} + \frac{1}{2} = 1$) on separate small sections of paper and have the child glue across the bottom of the paper to create a math problem that he or she can retell.

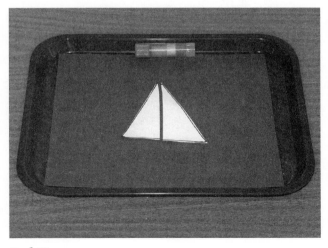

3rd Tray

Task 22

Three Pieces Make a Whole

Materials:

- Three plastic rectangular trays
- White paper to fit tray
- Colored pencils
- Square stencil
- Scissors
- Construction paper to fit tray
- Glue stick

Setup:

1. Place three trays in a horizontal row
2. Place colored pencils in a small container to the left of the first tray
3. **1st Tray:** Place white paper and stencil on the tray
4. **2nd Tray:** Place scissors either in an individual holder or across the top of the tray
5. **3rd Tray:** Place colored paper with glue stick at top of tray

1st Tray

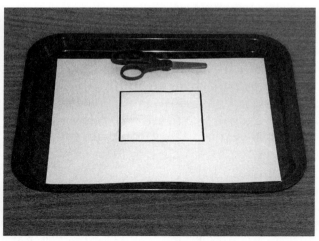

2nd Tray

Task:

1. **Beginning:** The goal is for the child to trace the square shape on white paper.
2. **Middle:** The goal is to move the shape to the second tray and cut the shape. Then, the child will cut the shape into three pieces.
3. **End:** The goal is for the child to transfer the three pieces of the square shape to the 3rd tray. Then, reassemble onto the colored construction paper using the glue stick so that it resembles the original geometric shape that was traced.

Outcome:

Child learns that three pieces of a shape make a whole shape again when reassembled.

Emerging Skills:

The child will practice following complex instructions of tracing, cutting, and assembling to form a square shape.

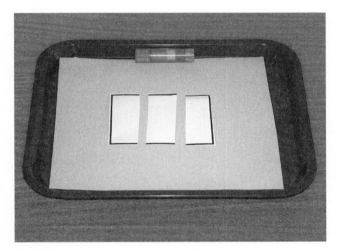

3rd Tray

Task 23

Four Pieces Make a Whole

⦚ *Materials:*

- Three plastic rectangular trays
- White paper to fit tray
- Colored pencils
- Rectangle stencil
- Scissors
- Construction paper to fit tray
- Glue stick

⦚ *Setup:*

1. Place three trays in a horizontal row
2. Place colored pencils in small container to the left of the first tray
3. **1st Tray:** Place white paper and stencil on the tray
4. **2nd Tray:** Place scissors either in an individual holder or across the top of the tray
5. **3rd Tray:** Place colored paper on 3rd tray with glue stick at top of tray

1st Tray

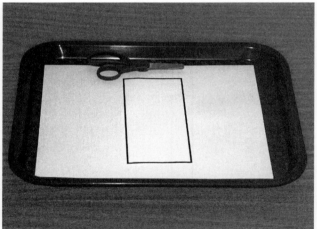

2nd Tray

Task:

1. **Beginning:** The goal is for the child to trace the shape on white paper.
2. **Middle:** The goal is to place the shape on the tray and cut out the shape. Then, child is to cut that shape into four pieces.
3. **End:** The goal is for the child to place the four pieces onto the colored paper and using the glue stick, reassemble the pieces into the original geometric shape.

Outcome:

The child learns that four pieces of a shape make a whole shape again when reassembled.

Emerging Skills:

The child will trace a familiar shape and problem solve how to fit pieces of that shape back into the original form.

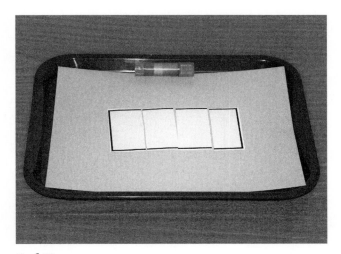

3rd Tray

Task 24

Five Pieces Make a Whole

≋ Materials:

- Three plastic rectangular trays
- White paper to fit tray
- Colored pencils
- Cross stencil
- Scissors
- Construction paper to fit tray
- Glue stick

≋ Setup:

1. Place three trays in a horizontal row
2. Place colored pencils in a small container to the left of the tray.
3. **1st Tray:** Place white paper and stencil on the tray
4. **2nd Tray:** Place scissors either in an individual holder or across the top of the tray
5. **3rd Tray:** Place colored paper on tray with a glue stick at top of tray

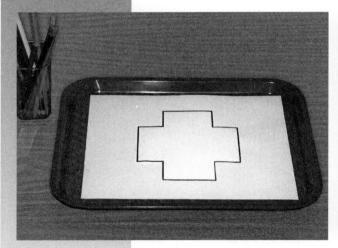

1st Tray

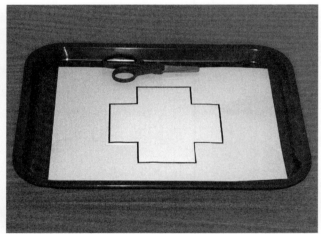

2nd Tray

⋙ Task:

1. **Beginning:** The goal is for the child to use a colored pencil and trace the shape onto the paper.
2. **Middle:** The goal is for the child to place the traced shape on the 2nd tray and cut out the shape. The child is to then cut the shape into five pieces.
3. **End:** The goal is for the child to place the five pieces of the shape onto the colored paper on the 3rd tray and use the glue stick to reassemble and glue to the paper.

⋙ Outcome:

Child learns that five pieces of a shape make a whole shape again when reassembled.

⋙ Emerging Skills:

The child develops an understanding of parts to a whole and applies this information to the parts-to-a-whole tasks.

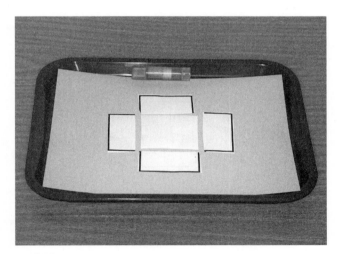

3rd Tray

Task 25

Six Pieces Make a Whole

░ Materials:

- Three plastic rectangular trays
- White paper to fit tray
- Colored pencils
- Hexagon stencil
- Scissors
- Construction paper to fit tray
- Glue stick

░ Setup:

1. Place three trays in a horizontal row
2. Place colored pencils in a small container to the left of the tray
3. **1st Tray:** Place white paper and shape on the tray
4. **2nd Tray:** Place scissors either in an individual holder or across the top of the tray
5. **3rd Tray:** Place colored paper on tray with a glue stick at top of tray

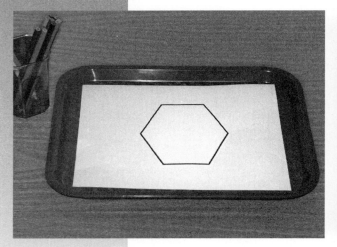

1st Tray

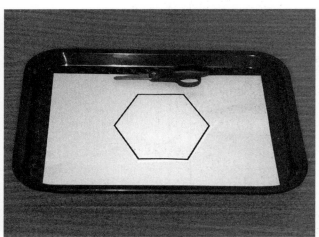

2nd Tray

Task:

1. **Beginning:** The goal is for the child to use a colored pencil and trace the shape.
2. **Middle:** The goal is for the child to place the traced shape on the 2nd tray and cut out the shape. The child is to then cut the shape into six sections.
3. **End:** The goal is for the child to place the six pieces of the geometric shape onto the colored paper on the 3rd tray, and using the glue stick, reassemble and glue to the paper.

Outcome:

The child learns that six pieces of a shape make a whole shape again when reassembled.

Emerging Skills:

The child begins to understand the math skill of fractions and sees that six equal parts make a whole.

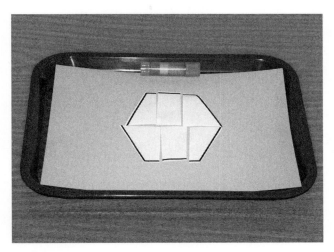

3rd Tray

Task 26

Seven Pieces Make a Whole

Materials:

- Three plastic rectangular trays
- White paper to fit tray
- Colored pencils
- Square stencil
- Scissors
- Construction paper to fit tray
- Glue stick

Setup:

1. Place three trays in a horizontal row
2. Place colored pencils in a small container to the left of the first tray
3. **1st Tray:** Place white paper and square stencil on the tray
4. **2nd Tray:** Place scissors either in an individual holder or across top of tray
5. **3rd Tray:** Place colored paper on tray with a glue stick at top of tray

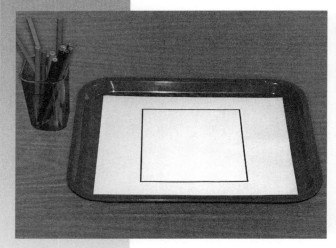

1st Tray

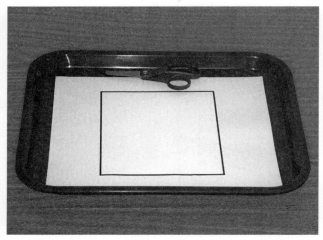

2nd Tray

Task:

1. **Beginning:** The goal is for the child to use a colored pencil and trace the shape.
2. **Middle:** The goal is for the child to place the traced shape on the 2nd tray and cut out the shape. The child is to then cut the shape into seven sections.
3. **End:** The goal is for the child to place the seven pieces onto the colored paper, and using the glue stick, reassemble and glue to the paper to create the original shape.

Outcome:

The child learns that seven pieces of a shape make a whole shape again when reassembled.

Emerging Skills:

This task provides the child with the opportunity to refine small muscle control, use arm and wrist movements, and enhance eye/hand coordination.

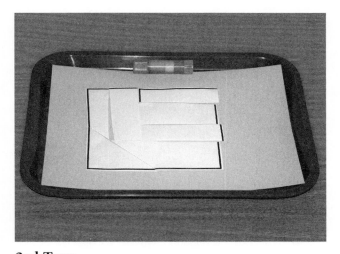

3rd Tray

Task 27

Eight Pieces Make a Whole

))) Materials:

- Three plastic rectangular trays
- White paper to fit tray
- Colored pencils
- Circle stencil
- Scissors
- Construction paper to fit tray
- Glue stick

))) Setup:

1. Place three trays in a horizontal row
2. Place colored pencils in a small container to the left of the first tray
3. **1st Tray:** Place white paper and shape on the tray
4. **2nd Tray:** Place scissors either in an individual holder or across top of tray
5. **3rd Tray:** Place colored paper on tray with a glue stick at top of tray

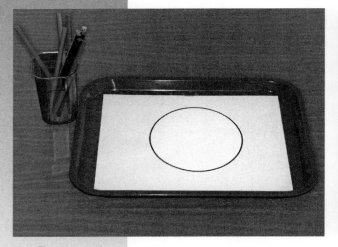

1st Tray

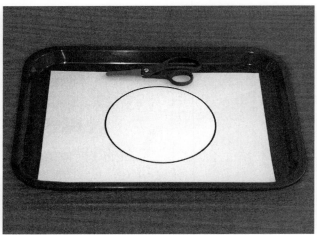

2nd Tray

Task:

1. **Beginning:** The goal is for the child to use a colored pencil and trace the shape.
2. **Middle:** The goal is for the child to place the traced shape on the 2nd tray and cut out the shape. The child is to then cut the shape into eight sections.
3. **End:** The goal is for the child to place the eight pieces onto the colored paper on the 3rd tray, and using the glue stick, reassemble and glue to the paper to recreate the original shape.

 ## Outcome:

The child learns that eight pieces of a shape make a whole shape again when reassembled.

 ## Emerging Skills:

The child practices counting to eight when reassembling pieces to create a whole circle again.

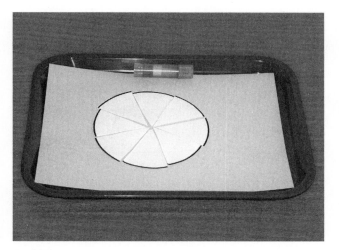

3rd Tray

Task 28

Nine Pieces Make a Whole

Materials:

- Three plastic rectangular trays
- White paper to fit tray
- Colored pencils
- Rectangle stencil
- Scissors
- Construction paper to fit tray
- Glue stick

Setup:

1. Place three trays in a horizontal row
2. Place colored pencils in a small container to the left of the first tray
3. **1st Tray:** Place white paper and shape on the tray
4. **2nd Tray:** Place scissors either in an individual holder or across top of tray
5. **3rd Tray:** Place colored paper on tray with a glue stick at top of tray

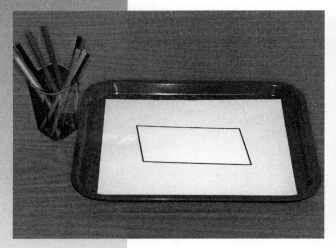

1st Tray

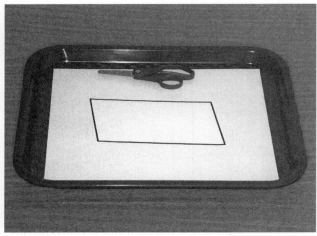

2nd Tray

Task:

1. **Beginning:** The goal is for the child to use a colored pencil and trace the shape.
2. **Middle:** The goal is for the child to place the traced shape on the 2nd tray and cut out the shape. The child is to then cut the shape into nine sections.
3. **End:** The goal is for the child to place the nine pieces onto the colored paper on the 3rd tray, reassemble into the original shape, and glue to the paper.

Outcome:

The child learns that nine pieces of a shape make a whole shape again when reassembled.

Emerging Skills:

The child is using problem-solving skills and decision making when reassembling to be sure all pieces recreate the same beginning shape.

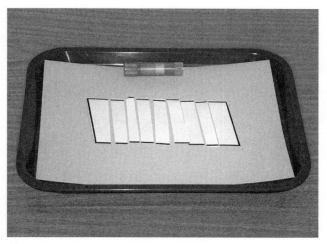

3rd Tray

Task 29

Ten Pieces Make a Whole

⫸ *Materials:*

- Three plastic rectangular trays
- White paper to fit tray
- Colored pencils
- Octagon stencil
- Scissors
- Construction paper to fit tray
- Glue stick

⫸ *Setup:*

1. Place three trays in a horizontal row
2. Place colored pencils in a small container to the left of the first tray
3. **1st Tray:** Place white paper and shape on the tray
4. **2nd Tray:** Place scissors either in an individual holder or across top of tray
5. **3rd Tray:** Place colored paper on tray with a glue stick at top of tray

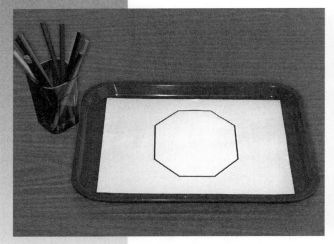

1st Tray

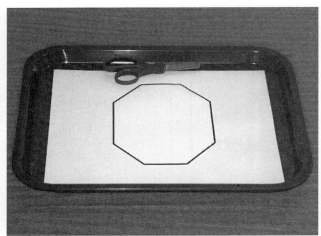

2nd Tray

Task:

1. **Beginning:** The goal is for the child to use a colored pencil and trace the shape.
2. **Middle:** The goal is for the child to place the traced shape on the 2nd tray and cut out the shape. The child is to then cut the shape into ten sections.
3. **End:** The goal is for the child to place the ten pieces onto the colored paper, and using the glue stick, reassemble and glue to the paper to create the original shape.

Outcome:

The child learns that ten pieces of a shape make a whole shape again when reassembled.

Emerging Skills:

The child uses his or her counting skills to be sure all pieces are included to make the original shape.

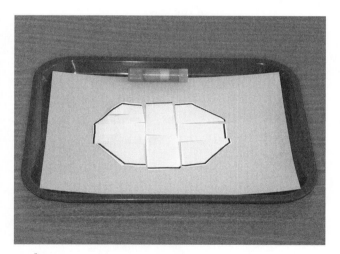

3rd Tray

SECTION IV—SEQUENCE—TRACE OR DRAW, CUT, AND ASSEMBLE

Task 30

Above and Below

Directional actions help a child develop a sense of spatial relationships. Using the tasks in this section, emphasize spatial relations such as sequencing tasks. Sequencing tasks provide experience in learning opposite, directional, and positional words.

※ Materials:

- Three plastic rectangular trays
- White paper to fit tray
- Thin black marker
- Small triangle and small circle stencil
- Scissors
- Construction paper to fit tray with a line drawn horizontally across the middle of the paper
- Glue stick

※ Setup:

1. Place three trays in a horizontal row
2. **1st Tray:** Place white paper and marker on tray
3. **2nd Tray:** Place scissors across the top of the tray
4. **3rd Tray:** Place colored paper with a horizontal line drawn across the middle of the paper on the tray with a glue stick at the top of the tray

1st Tray

2nd Tray

Task:

1. **Beginning:** The goal is for the child to trace both the circle and the triangle shapes onto the white paper using a thin black marker.
2. **Middle:** The goal is for the child to transfer the traced paper to the 2nd tray and use the scissors to cut out the two shapes.
3. **End:** The goal is for the child to transfer the cut shapes to the 3rd tray and glue the circle above the line and the triangle below the line.

Outcome:

The child learns to follow directions and glues shapes onto paper in their correct positions (circle above the line and triangle below the line).

Emerging Skills:

The child is learning to retain information while practicing decision making to solve the task problem.

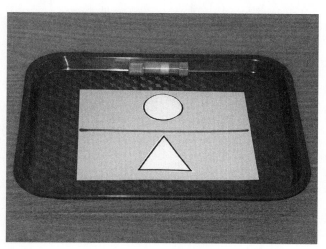

3rd Tray

Task 31

Beginning, Middle, and End

))) Materials:

- Three rectangular trays
- One small square each of blue, red, and yellow construction paper
- Black marker
- Small square stencil
- White paper to fit the size of the tray
- Scissors
- Glue stick

))) Setup:

1. Place three trays in a horizontal row
2. **1st Tray:** Place three small sheets of colored construction paper on tray with black marker at top of tray. The order of the sheet colors are blue, red, and then yellow.
3. **2nd Tray:** Place scissors across the top of the tray
4. **3rd Tray:** Place white paper on tray with a glue stick at top of the tray

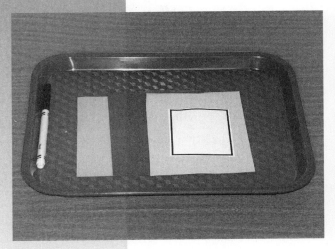

1st Tray

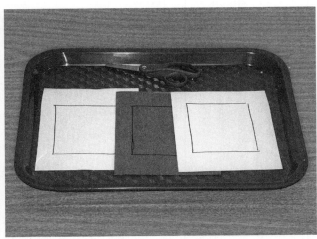

2nd Tray

Task:

1. **Beginning:** The goal is for the child to trace a square shape on each of the three colors of paper.
2. **Middle:** The goal is for the child to place the three colored squares on the 2nd tray and cut them out.
3. **End:** The goal is for the child to glue the three colored squares in a row on the white paper starting with the blue, then red, then yellow.

Outcome:

The child determines the order of what is glued by remembering the order they were traced and cut.

Emerging Skills:

The child develops short-term memory experience when recalling the order of the squares.

Extension Activity:

Ask any of these follow-up tasks:

- Ask the child to point to the beginning color square, the middle color square, and the end color square
- Ask the child to label each square with ready-made label words for beginning, middle, and end that you have prepared
- Ask the child to circle the beginning square, to put an X through the middle square, and then to draw a picture on the end square

3rd Tray

Task 32

Big and Little

⫸ Materials:

- Three rectangular trays
- White paper
- Black crayon
- A large square and a small square stencil
- Scissors
- Construction paper to fit tray
- Glue stick
- Word labels for big and little (optional)

⫸ Setup:

1. Place three trays in a horizontal row
2. **1st Tray:** Place white paper and stencils on the tray with the black crayon on the left side of the tray
3. **2nd Tray:** Place scissors across the top of tray
4. **3rd Tray:** Place colored paper on tray with a glue stick at top of tray

1st Tray

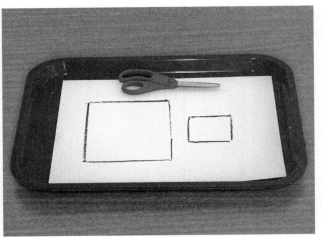

2nd Tray

Task:

1. **Beginning:** The goal is for the child to trace two shapes on the white paper with the black crayon.
2. **Middle:** The goal is for the child to place the white paper onto the 2nd tray and cut out shapes.
3. **End:** The goal is for the child to place the two cut-out shapes on the 3rd tray, and using the glue stick, organize the shapes by gluing the shape that is big first; then glue the shape that is little next to it on the paper.

 ## Outcome:

The child determines which traced shapes are glued in what order.

 ## Emerging Skills:

The child experiences decision making when identifying size differences. The child must determine the size differences to successfully complete the task.

Extension Activity:

Teacher may ask the child to use word labels of big and little and glue onto the correct shape.

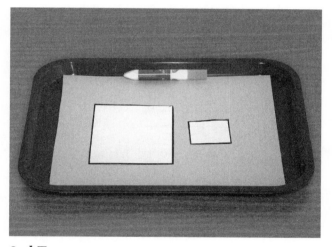

3rd Tray

Task 33

First, Second, and Third

))) Materials:

- Three rectangular trays
- White paper with arrows
- Yellow highlighter pen
- Rectangle stencil
- Scissors
- Construction paper to fit tray
- Glue stick
- Ordinal number labels (optional)

))) Setup:

1. Place three trays in a horizontal row
2. **1st Tray:** Place arrow sheet on tray with yellow highlighter
3. **2nd Tray:** Place scissors across top of tray
4. **3rd Tray:** Place colored paper on tray with a glue stick at top of tray

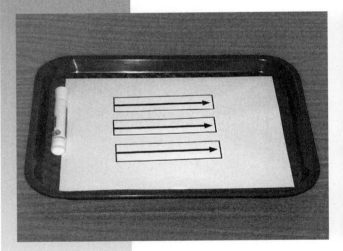

1st Tray

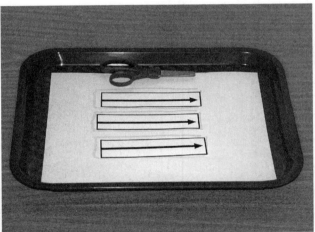

2nd Tray

Task:

1. **Beginning:** The goal is for the child to highlight the outline of the rectangle around each of the three arrows using the yellow highlighter.
2. **Middle:** The goal is for the child to place the highlighted arrows sheet on the 2nd tray and cut along the highlighted lines to create three arrows inside rectangles shapes.
3. **End:** The goal is for the child to glue the three arrow shapes according to the following teacher examples:

   1st – Glue the first rectangle so the arrow is pointing up

   2nd – Glue the second rectangle so the arrow is pointing down

   3rd – Glue the third rectangle so the arrow is pointing away from the rest of the trays

Outcome:

The child determines the order sequence of the arrows by remembering the instructions.

Emerging Skills:

To experience decision making when choosing which arrows are to face which direction.

Extension Activity:

The following extension activities are presented as a challenge for the child who possesses an understanding of ordinal positions.

- Prepare symbol labels 1st, 2nd, and 3rd for child to glue onto arrows
- Child labels each arrow by writing 1st, 2nd, 3rd beside, below, or on the appropriate arrow

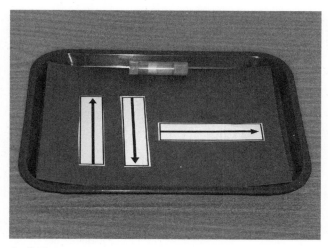

3rd Tray

Task 34

In Front of
and
Next to

⧼ *Materials:*

- Three rectangular trays
- White paper to fit the tray
- One large rectangle and two small triangle stencils
- Thin black marker
- Scissors
- Construction paper to fit tray
- Glue stick

⧼ *Setup:*

1. Place three trays in a horizontal row
2. **1st Tray:** Place white paper, stencils, and thin black marker on tray
3. **2nd Tray:** Place scissors across top of the tray
4. **3rd Tray:** Place colored paper on tray with a glue stick at the top of the tray

1st Tray

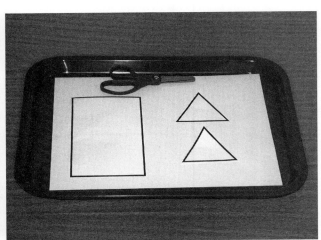

2nd Tray

⁂ Task:

1. **Beginning:** The goal is for the child to trace the large rectangle shape and the two small triangle shapes.
2. **Middle:** The goal is for the child to transfer the traced paper to the 2nd tray and use the scissors to cut out the three shapes.
3. **End:** The goal is for the child to transfer the large rectangle to the 3rd tray and glue onto the middle of the paper. Then, transfer the two smaller triangle shapes to the tray gluing one *in front of* the large rectangle and the other one *next to* the large rectangle.

⁂ Outcome:

The child is able to visualize the smaller triangle placement in front of and next to the rectangle.

⁂ Emerging Skills:

The child is increasing listening skills as he or she remembers during problem solving to place triangles in their proper positions in front of or next to the large rectangle.

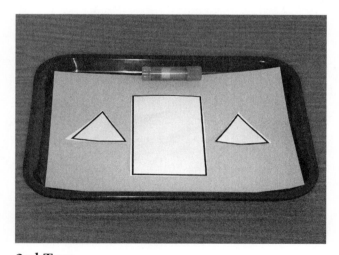

3rd Tray

Task 35

Layered

Materials:

- Three rectangular trays
- White paper to fit tray
- Black crayon
- Large rectangle, medium circle, and small triangle stencils
- Scissors
- Construction paper to fit tray
- Glue stick

Setup:

1. Place three trays in a horizontal row
2. **1st Tray:** Place white paper on tray and black crayon on the left side of the tray. Place large rectangle, medium circle, and small triangle stencils on paper.
3. **2nd Tray:** Place scissors across top of tray
4. **3rd Tray:** Place one sheet of colored construction paper on the tray with the glue stick across top of the tray

1st Tray

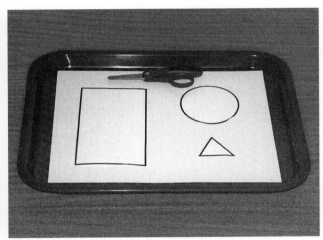

2nd Tray

Task:

1. **Beginning:** The goal is for the child to trace each of the three shapes.
2. **Middle:** The goal is for the child to transfer the traced paper to the 2nd tray and cut out all three shapes.
3. **End:** The goal is for the child to glue one shape on top of the other starting with the large rectangle, then the medium circle, and then the small triangle.

Outcome:

The child correctly glues shapes in a layering pattern.

Emerging Skills:

The child uses visual discrimination skills to determine which shape is glued first, next, and last.

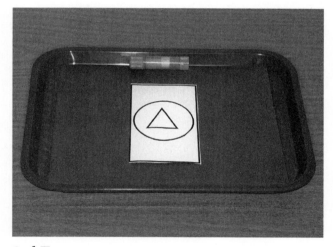

3rd Tray

Task 36

Left and Right

〰 *Materials:*

- Three rectangular trays
- White paper to fit the tray
- Black crayon
- Scissors
- Construction paper to fit tray
- Glue stick

〰 *Setup:*

1. Place three trays in a horizontal row
2. **1st Tray:** Place white paper on tray with black crayon on the left side of the tray
3. **2nd Tray:** Place scissors across the top of the tray
4. **3rd Tray:** Place colored construction paper horizontally creasing it to resemble pages in a book and laying it flat on the tray

1st Tray

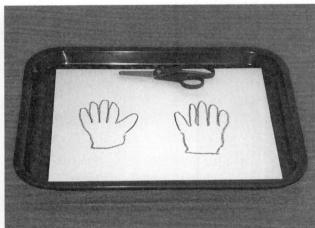

2nd Tray

⧙ Task:

1. **Beginning:** The goal is for the child to trace one of his or her hands two times on the white paper with the black crayon.

2. **Middle:** The goal is for the child to transfer the drawn hands to the 2nd tray and cut them out.

3. **End:** The goal is for the child to glue each hand in its correct placement, left hand on the left side of the creased paper, the right hand on the right side of the creased paper. (Hints: The child is to turn over one of the hands so that the thumbs face each other. Also, for younger children, the teacher can draw a line down the crease and designate right and left sides by labeling the paper.)

⧙ Outcome:

The child reinforces left and right positions.

⧙ Emerging Skills:

The child increases fine motor skills of tracing and cutting while determining the directions of left and right.

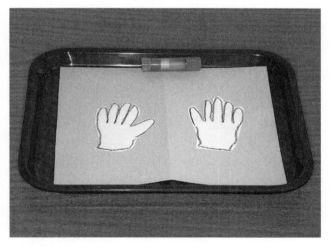

3rd Tray

Task 37

On and Off

))) Materials:

- Three rectangular trays
- White paper to fit the tray
- Thin black marker
- Large square and two small circle stencils
- Scissors
- Construction paper to fit the tray
- Glue stick
- Word labels (optional)

))) Setup:

1. Place three trays in a horizontal row
2. **1st Tray:** Place one large square and two small circle shape stencils on white paper. Place marker on the side of the tray
3. **2nd Tray:** Place scissors across top of the tray
4. **3rd Tray:** Place construction paper on tray with a glue stick across top of tray

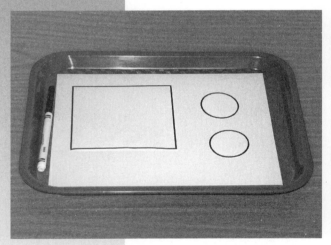

1st Tray

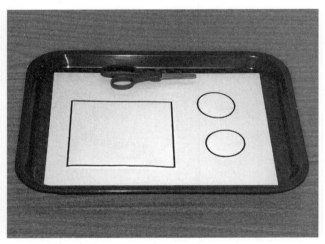

2nd Tray

⫸ Task:

1. **Beginning:** The goal is for the child to trace one large square shape and two small circles.

2. **Middle:** The goal is for the child to place the traced shape paper on the 2nd tray and cut out all three shapes.

3. **End:** The goal is for the child to first glue the large square shape in the middle of the paper. Then, add the small circle shapes according to the following instructions:
   - glue one small circle *on* the square
   - glue one small circle *off* the square

⫸ Outcome:

The child demonstrates the understanding of on and off.

⫸ Emerging Skills:

The child experiences decision making when determining the positioning of circles in relationship to the square.

⫸ Extension Activity:

The following extension activity is presented as a challenge for the child who possesses an understanding of positional words.
   - Child can identify each circle by labeling one *on* and the other *off* using word labels

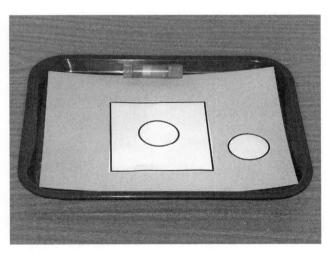

3rd Tray

Task 38

Young and Old

))) Materials:

- Three rectangular trays
- Magazines
- Scissors
- Construction paper to fit tray
- Glue stick

))) Setup:

1. Place three trays in a horizontal row
2. **1st Tray:** Place a magazine or ready-to-cut pictures on tray
3. **2nd Tray:** Place scissors across top of the tray
4. **3rd Tray:** Place colored paper on tray with a glue stick at top of tray

1st Tray

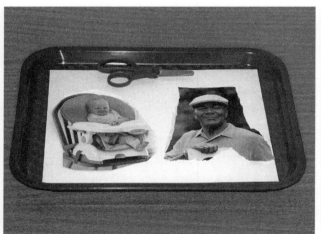

2nd Tray

Task:

1. **Beginning:** The goal is for the child to select two pictures from a magazine that represent people that are young and old. Child is to tear pictures from the magazine.

2. **Middle:** The goal is for the child to place the pictures on the 2nd tray and cut around each picture.

3. **End:** The goal is for the child to place the two cut-out pictures on the 3rd tray. Using the glue stick, organize the pictures gluing the picture representing young, then the picture representing old next to each other on the paper.

Outcome:

The child reinforces the concept of young and old when demonstrating knowledge by the correct placement of the pictures.

Emerging Skills:

The child demonstrates an understanding of young and old which helps build an anti-bias awareness.

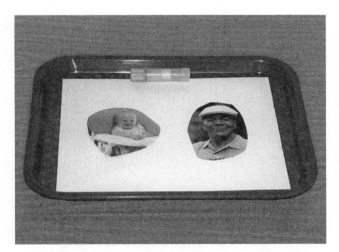

3rd Tray

SECTION V—LETTERS—TRACE OR WRITE, CUT, AND ASSEMBLE

Task 39

Letter of the Week

This section provides children with the opportunity to increase awareness of letter recognition. The tasks include practice in identifying uppercase and lowercase letters as well as building self-esteem when recognizing and identifying letters in the children's own names.

Check with your local school districts to find out which type of manuscript is taught in your area.

Materials:

- Three plastic rectangular trays
- White paper to fit the tray
- Uppercase and lowercase letter stencils made by teacher or store-bought
- A primary pencil
- Scissors
- Construction paper to fit tray
- Glue stick

Setup:

1. Place three trays in a horizontal row
2. **1st Tray:** Place white paper on tray and pencil across the top of the tray. Scatter letters to the left of the first tray.
3. **2nd Tray:** Place scissors across the top of the tray
4. **3rd Tray:** Place colored paper on tray with a glue stick at the top of the tray

1st Tray

2nd Tray

Task:

1. **Beginning:** The goal is for the child to sort through the letters to find an uppercase and lowercase letter representing your letter of the week and trace each onto the paper.
2. **Middle:** The goal is for the child to transfer the traced paper to the 2nd tray and cut out the letters.
3. **End:** The goal is for the child to glue the traced letters onto paper in the order of uppercase then lowercase.

Outcome:

The child is able to correctly recognize a particular letter as well as determine the uppercase and lowercase for the letter.

Emerging Skills:

The child applies letter recognition skills to this task while comprehending that every letter has an uppercase and lowercase.

3rd Tray

Task 40

First Letter of First Name

⁂ Materials:

- Three plastic rectangular trays
- White paper to fit the tray
- Uppercase letter stencils either made by teacher or store-bought
- A primary pencil
- Scissors
- Construction paper to fit tray
- Glue stick

⁂ Setup:

1. Place three trays in a horizontal row
2. **1st Tray:** Place white paper on tray with pencil on the left side. Scatter letters beside the tray.
3. **2nd Tray:** Place scissors across the top of the tray
4. **3rd Tray:** Place colored paper on tray with a glue stick at the top of the tray

1st Tray

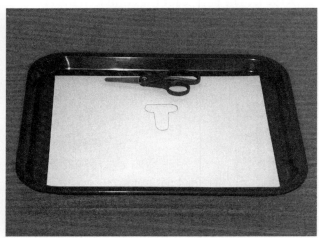

2nd Tray

⟩⟩⟩ *Task:*

1. **Beginning:** The goal is for the child to sort through the uppercase letters to find the letter that begins his or her first name and then trace the letter onto the paper.
2. **Middle:** The goal is for the child to transfer the traced paper to the 2nd tray and cut out the letter.
3. **End:** The goal is for the child to glue the traced letter onto paper.

⟩⟩⟩ *Outcome:*

The child enhances his or her self-esteem in recognizing and identifying the beginning letter of his or her first name.

⟩⟩⟩ *Emerging Skills:*

The child develops alphabetic awareness and continues to develop the ability to coordinate motions to hold and cut paper at the same time.

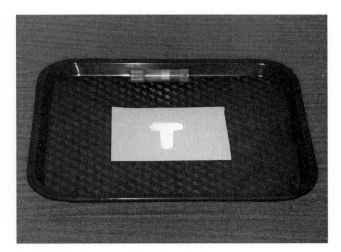

3rd Tray

Task 41

First Letter of Last Name

🎇 Materials:

- Three plastic rectangular trays
- White paper to fit the tray
- Uppercase letter stencils either made by teacher or store-bought
- A primary pencil
- Scissors
- Construction paper to fit tray
- Glue stick

🎇 Setup:

1. Place three trays in a horizontal row
2. **1st Tray:** Place white paper on tray with pencil on left side of tray. Scatter letters to the left of the tray.
3. **2nd Tray:** Place scissors across the top of the tray
4. **3rd Tray:** Place colored paper on tray with a glue stick at the top of the tray

1st Tray

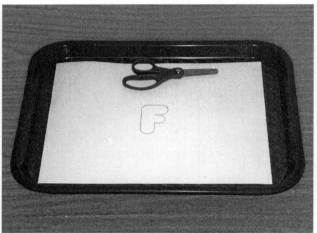

2nd Tray

Task:

1. **Beginning:** The goal is for the child to sort through the uppercase letters to find the first letter that begins his or her last name and then trace the letter onto the paper.
2. **Middle:** The goal is for the child to transfer the traced paper to the 2nd tray and cut out the letter.
3. **End:** The goal is for the child to glue the traced letter onto paper.

Outcome:

The child builds his or her self-esteem in recognizing and identifying the first letter of his or her last name.

Emerging Skills:

The child develops alphabetic awareness when recognizing the beginning letter of his or her last name.

3rd Tray

Task 42

Letters We Love

⧘ Materials:

- Three plastic rectangular trays
- White paper to fit tray
- Lowercase letter stencils made by teacher or store-bought
- A primary pencil
- Scissors
- Construction paper to fit tray
- Glue stick

⧘ Setup:

1. Place three trays in a horizontal row
2. **1st Tray:** Place white paper on tray and pencil across the top of the tray. Scatter letters to the left of the tray.
3. **2nd Tray:** Place scissors across the top of the tray
4. **3rd Tray:** Place colored paper on tray with a glue stick at the top of the tray

1st Tray

2nd Tray

Task:

1. **Beginning:** The goal is for the child to sort through the letters and choose letters that match a three-letter word determined by the teacher and trace them.
2. **Middle:** The goal is for the child to transfer the traced paper to the 2nd tray and cut out the letters.
3. **End:** The goal is for the child to glue the traced letters onto paper in the proper sequence to create a three-letter word.

Outcome:

The child correctly cuts and glues letters in the proper sequence to form a three-letter word.

Emerging Skills:

The child learns how to sequence a three-letter word. He or she also identifies letters and how they are used to create words we love.

Extension Activity:

The following extension activities are presented as a challenge for the child who possesses an understanding of letter-to-sound identification:

- Ask child to print the letters below the glued ones and say letters aloud
- Ask child to sound out the letters to say the word
- Ask child to draw a picture to match the word
- Ask child to match letter stencils to the cut-out letters when the word is finished

3rd Tray

Task 43

Sticks and Circles Letters

))) Materials:

- Three plastic rectangular trays
- White paper with squares drawn on the paper (adult needs to draw squares on each paper depending on the number of letters in each child's first name)
- A primary pencil
- Scissors
- Construction paper to fit tray
- Glue stick

))) Setup:

1. Place three trays in a horizontal row
2. Place letters in a container to the left of the first tray
3. **1st Tray:** Place white paper with drawn squares on tray along with a pencil on the left side of the tray
4. **2nd Tray:** Place scissors across the top of the tray
5. **3rd Tray:** Place colored paper on tray with a glue stick at the top of the tray

1st Tray

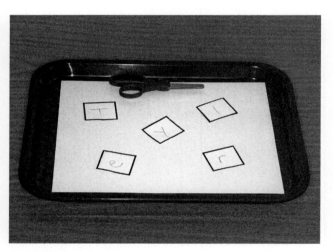

2nd Tray

Task:

1. **Beginning:** The goal is for the child to write his or her first name putting one letter in each square.
2. **Middle:** The goal is for the child to transfer the traced paper to the 2nd tray and cut out the letter squares.
3. **End:** The goal is for the child to glue the letter squares in the correct order of the first name.

Outcome:

The child feels good about recognizing the letters of his or her first name and builds confidence in writing the letters of his or her first name by gluing them in order.

Emerging Skills:

The child develops a sense of print awareness, recognizes name, and identifies letter formations.

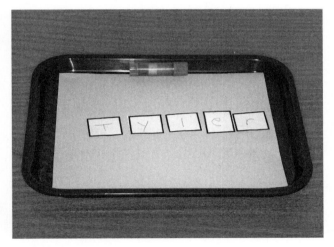

3rd Tray

Task 44

Letter Outlines

※ Materials:

- Three plastic rectangular trays
- White paper containing a horizontal rectangle
- A primary pencil
- Scissors
- Construction paper to fit tray
- Glue stick

※ Setup:

1. Place three trays in a horizontal row
2. **1st Tray:** Place paper with drawn rectangle on tray and place pencil on the left side of tray
3. **2nd Tray:** Place scissors across the top of the tray
4. **3rd Tray:** Place colored paper on tray with a glue stick at the top of the tray

1st Tray

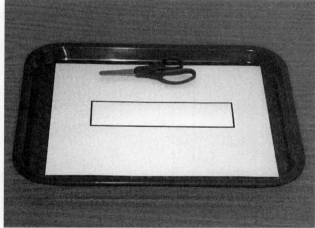

2nd Tray

Task:

1. **Beginning:** The goal is for the child to write his or her first name inside the rectangle outline.
2. **Middle:** The goal is for the child to transfer the traced paper to the 2nd tray and cut out the rectangle.
3. **End:** The goal is for the child to glue the traced rectangle onto paper.

Outcome:

The child will correctly write his or her first name inside the rectangle outline.

Emerging Skills:

The child sequences uppercase and lowercase letters as he or she recognizes and writes the letters of the first name.

3rd Tray

SECTION VI—NUMBERS— TRACE, CUT, AND ASSEMBLE

Task 45

Number One and One Shape

This section provides information on how to create three-step tray tasks that reinforce the concept of how many with numerals. The tasks include numerals 1 through 10. For advanced students, teachers may extend to 20.

Materials:

- Three plastic rectangular trays
- Small container to hold paper numeral squares and paper shapes
- White paper to fit tray
- Small circle stencil
- Numerals 1–10 each written in squares
- A primary pencil
- Scissors
- Construction paper to fit tray
- Glue stick

Setup:

1. Place three trays in a horizontal row
2. Place stencil and numerals in a container to the left of the first tray
3. **1st Tray:** Place white paper on tray and pencil on the left sides of the tray
4. **2nd Tray:** Place scissors across the top of the tray
5. **3rd Tray:** Place colored paper on tray with a glue stick at the top of the tray

1st Tray

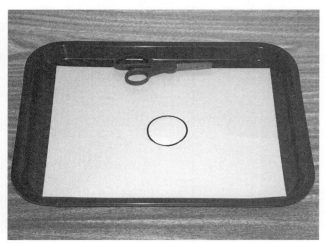

2nd Tray

Task:

1. **Beginning:** The goal is for the child to sort through numerals and find number 1, select the shape, and trace it on the paper one time.
2. **Middle:** The goal is for the child to transfer the traced paper to the 2nd tray and cut out the shape.
3. **End:** The goal is for the child to glue one shape and the numeral square below the shape.

Outcome:

The child recognizes the number 1 and how many shapes are needed for that number.

Emerging Skills:

The child understands numeral awareness as he or she develops a sense of how many the numeral represents.

Extension Activity:

The following extension activity is presented as a challenge for the child who possesses an understanding of number symbols.

- Child writes the number to represent how many shapes are on the paper

3rd Tray

Task 46

Number Two and Two Shapes

⅏ Materials:

- Three plastic rectangular trays
- Small container to hold paper numeral squares and paper shapes
- White paper to fit tray
- Small circle stencil
- Numerals 1–10 each written in squares
- A primary pencil
- Scissors
- Construction paper to fit tray
- Glue stick

⅏ Setup:

1. Place three trays in a horizontal row
2. Place circle stencil and numerals in a container to the left of the first tray
3. **1st Tray:** Place white paper on tray and pencil on the left side of the tray
4. **2nd Tray:** Place scissors across the top of the tray
5. **3rd Tray:** Place colored paper on tray with a glue stick at the top of the tray

1st Tray

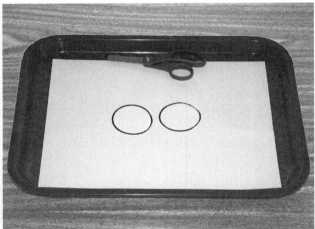

2nd Tray

Task:

1. **Beginning:** The goal is for the child to sort through numerals and find number 2 and trace the circle shape two times on the paper.
2. **Middle:** The goal is for the child to transfer the traced paper to the 2nd tray and cut out the shapes.
3. **End:** The goal is for the child to glue the circle shapes in a row and glue the numeral square below the shapes.

Outcome:

The child recognizes the number 2 and traces that many circles to represent the number.

Emerging Skills:

The child develops numeral awareness and a sense of how many the numeral represents.

Extension Activity:

The following extension activity is presented as a challenge for the child who possesses an understanding of number symbols.

- Child writes the number to represent how many shapes are on the paper

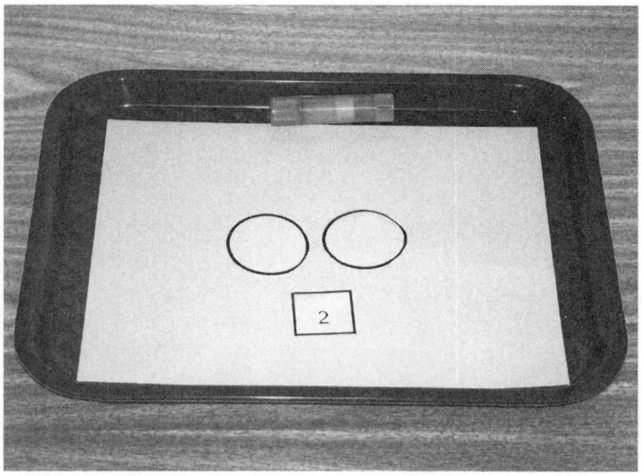

3rd Tray

Task 47

Number Three and Three Shapes

∭ Materials:

- Three plastic rectangular trays
- Small container to hold paper numeral squares and paper shapes
- White paper to fit tray
- Small circle stencil
- Numerals 1–10 each written in squares
- A primary pencil
- Scissors
- Construction paper to fit tray
- Glue stick

∭ Setup:

1. Place three trays in a horizontal row
2. Place circle stencil and numerals in a container to the left of the first tray
3. **1st Tray:** Place white paper on tray and the pencil on the left side of the tray
4. **2nd Tray:** Place scissors across the top of the tray
5. **3rd Tray:** Place colored paper on tray with a glue stick at the top of the tray

1st Tray

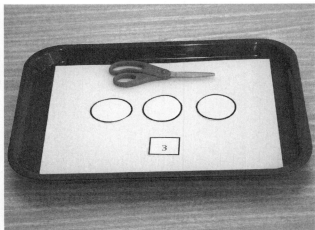

2nd Tray

Task:

1. **Beginning:** The goal is for the child to sort through numerals and find number 3 and trace the circle shape that many times on the paper.
2. **Middle:** The goal is for the child to transfer the traced paper to the 2nd tray and cut out the shapes.
3. **End:** The goal is for the child to glue the shapes in a row and glue the numeral square below the shapes.

Outcome:

The child recognizes the number 3 and how many that number represents.

Emerging Skills:

The child develops numeral awareness and a sense of how many the numeral represents by counting the shapes.

Extension Activity:

The following extension activity is presented as a challenge for the child who possesses an understanding of number symbols.

● Child writes the number to represent how many shapes are on the paper

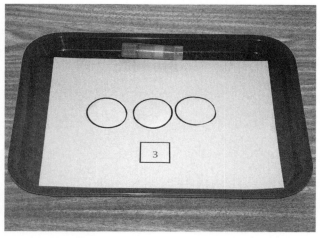

3rd Tray

Task 48

Number Four and Four Shapes

⫸ *Materials:*

- Three plastic rectangular trays
- Small container to hold paper numeral squares and paper shapes
- White paper to fit tray
- Small circle stencil
- Numerals 1–10 each written in squares
- A primary pencil
- Scissors
- Construction paper to fit tray
- Glue stick

⫸ *Setup:*

1. Place three trays in a horizontal row
2. Place circle stencil and numerals in a container to the left of the first tray
3. **1st Tray:** Place white paper on tray and pencil on the left side of the tray
4. **2nd Tray:** Place scissors across the top of the tray
5. **3rd Tray:** Place colored paper on tray with a glue stick at the top of the tray

1st Tray

2nd Tray

Task:

1. **Beginning:** The goal is for the child to sort through numerals and find number 4 and trace the circle stencil that many times on the paper.
2. **Middle:** The goal is for the child to transfer the traced paper to the 2nd tray and cut out the shapes.
3. **End:** The goal is for the child to glue the shapes in a row and glue the numeral square below the shape.

 Outcome:

The child recognizes the number 4 and how many that number represents.

Emerging Skills:

The child develops numeral awareness and a sense of how many the numeral represents by counting the shapes.

Extension Activity:

The following extension activity is presented as a challenge for the child who possesses an understanding of number symbols.

- Child writes the number to represent how many shapes are on the paper

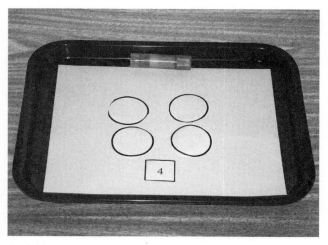

3rd Tray

Task 49

Number Five and Five Shapes

⅗ Materials:

- Three plastic rectangular trays
- Small container to hold paper numeral squares and circle stencil
- White paper to fit tray
- Small circle stencil
- Numerals 1–10 each written in squares
- A primary pencil
- Scissors
- Sheet of colored construction paper to fit tray
- Glue stick

⅗ Setup:

1. Place three trays in a horizontal row
2. Place circle stencil and numerals in a container to the left of the first tray
3. **1st Tray:** Place white paper on tray and pencil on the left side of tray
4. **2nd Tray:** Place scissors across the top of the tray
5. **3rd Tray:** Place colored paper on tray with a glue stick at the top of the tray

1st Tray

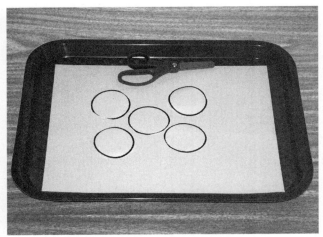

2nd Tray

⧼ Task:

1. **Beginning:** The goal is for the child to sort through numerals and find number 5 and trace the circle stencil that many times on the paper.
2. **Middle:** The goal is for the child to transfer the traced paper to the 2nd tray and cut out the shapes.
3. **End:** The goal is for the child to glue the shapes in a row and glue the numeral square below the shape.

⧼ Outcome:

The child recognizes the number 5 and how many that number represents.

⧼ Emerging Skills:

The child develops numeral awareness and a sense of how many the numeral represents.

⧼ Extension Activity:

The following extension activity is presented as a challenge for the child who possesses an understanding of number symbols.

● Child writes the number to represent how many shapes are on the paper

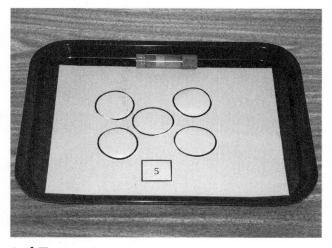

3rd Tray

Task 50

Number Six and Six Shapes

≋ Materials:

- Three plastic rectangular trays
- Small container to hold paper numeral squares and paper shapes
- White paper to fit tray
- Small circle stencil
- Numerals 1–10 each written in squares
- A primary pencil
- Scissors
- Construction paper to fit tray
- Glue stick

≋ Setup:

1. Place three trays in a horizontal row
2. Place circle stencil and numerals in a container to the left of the first tray
3. **1st Tray:** Place white paper on tray and pencil on the left side of tray
4. **2nd Tray:** Place scissors across the top of the tray
5. **3rd Tray:** Place colored paper on tray with a glue stick at the top of the tray

1st Tray

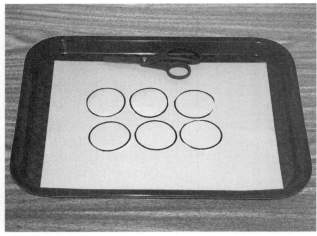

2nd Tray

⁂ Task:

1. **Beginning:** The goal is for the child to sort through numerals and find number 6 and trace six circle shapes on the paper.
2. **Middle:** The goal is for the child to transfer the traced paper to the 2nd tray and cut out the shapes.
3. **End:** The goal is for the child to glue the shapes in two rows and glue the numeral square below the shape.

⁂ Outcome:

The child recognizes the number 6 and how many that number represents by creating two rows of three each.

⁂ Emerging Skills:

The child develops numeral awareness and a sense of how many the numeral represents.

⁂ Extension Activity:

The following extension activity is presented as a challenge for the child who possesses an understanding of number symbols.

● Child writes the number to represent how many shapes are on the paper

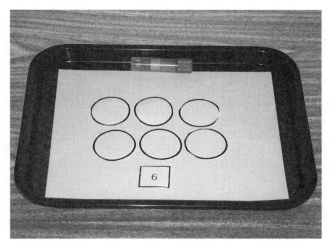

3rd Tray

Task 51

Number Seven and Seven Shapes

⚒ *Materials:*

- Three plastic rectangular trays
- Small container to hold paper numeral squares and paper shapes
- White paper to fit tray
- Small circle stencil
- Numerals 1–10 each written in squares
- A primary pencil
- Scissors
- Construction paper to fit tray
- Glue stick

⚒ *Setup:*

1. Place three trays in a horizontal row
2. Place circle stencil and numerals in a container to the left of the first tray
3. **1st Tray:** Place white paper on tray and pencil on left side of tray
4. **2nd Tray:** Place scissors across the top of the tray
5. **3rd Tray:** Place colored paper on tray with a glue stick at the top of the tray

1st Tray

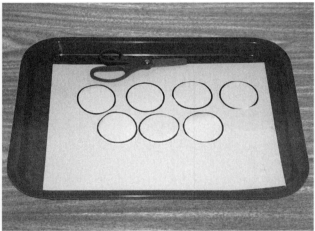

2nd Tray

Task:

1. **Beginning:** The goal is for the child to sort through numerals and find number 7 and trace seven circle shapes on the paper.
2. **Middle:** The goal is for the child to transfer the traced paper to the 2nd tray and cut out the shapes.
3. **End:** The goal is for the child to glue the shapes in two rows and glue the numeral square below the shape.

Outcome:

The child recognizes the number 7 and how many that number represents.

Emerging Skills:

The child develops numeral awareness and a sense of how many the numeral represents.

Extension Activity:

The following extension activity is presented as a challenge for the child who possesses an understanding of number symbols.

- Child writes the number to represent how many shapes are on the paper

3rd Tray

Task 52

Number Eight and Eight Shapes

⫸ Materials:

- Three plastic rectangular trays
- Small container to hold paper numeral squares and paper shapes
- White paper to fit tray
- Small circle stencil
- Numerals 1–10 each written in squares
- A primary pencil
- Scissors
- Construction paper to fit tray
- Glue stick

⫸ Setup:

1. Place three trays in a horizontal row
2. Place circle stencil and numerals in a container to the left of the first tray
3. **1st Tray:** Place white paper on tray and pencil on left side of tray
4. **2nd Tray:** Place scissors across the top of the tray
5. **3rd Tray:** Place colored paper on tray with a glue stick at the top of the tray

1st Tray

2nd Tray

))) Task:

1. **Beginning:** The goal is for the child to sort through numerals and find number 8 and trace eight circle shapes on the paper.
2. **Middle:** The goal is for the child to transfer the traced paper to the 2nd tray and cut out the shapes.
3. **End:** The goal is for the child to glue the shapes in two rows and glue the numeral square below the shape.

))) Outcome:

The child recognizes the number 8 and how many that number represents.

))) Emerging Skills:

The child develops numeral awareness and a sense of how many the numeral represents.

))) Extension Activity:

The following extension activity is presented as a challenge for the child who possesses an understanding of number symbols.

● Child writes the number to represent how many shapes are on the paper

3rd Tray

Task 53

Number Nine and Nine Shapes

⁑ Materials:

- Three plastic rectangular trays
- Small container to hold paper numeral squares and paper shapes
- White paper to fit tray
- Small circle stencil
- Numerals 1–10 each written in squares
- A primary pencil
- Scissors
- Construction paper to fit tray
- Glue stick

⁑ Setup:

1. Place three trays in a horizontal row
2. Place circle stencil and numerals in a container to the left of the first tray
3. **1st Tray:** Place white paper on tray and pencil on the left side of tray
4. **2nd Tray:** Place scissors across the top of the tray
5. **3rd Tray:** Place colored paper on tray with a glue stick at the top of the tray

1st Tray

2nd Tray

Task:

1. **Beginning:** The goal is for the child to sort through numerals and find number 9 and trace that many circles on the paper.
2. **Middle:** The goal is for the child to transfer the traced paper to the 2nd tray and cut out the shapes.
3. **End:** The goal is for the child to glue the shapes in two rows and glue the numeral square below the shape.

Outcome:

The child recognizes the number 9 and how many that number represents.

Emerging Skills:

The child develops numeral awareness and a sense of how many the numeral represents.

Extension Activity:

The following extension activity is presented as a challenge for the child who possesses an understanding of number symbols.

- Child writes the number to represent how many shapes are on the paper

3rd Tray

Task 54

Number Ten and Ten Shapes

Materials:

- Three plastic rectangular trays
- Small container to hold paper numeral squares and paper shapes
- White paper to fit tray
- Small circle stencil
- Numerals 1–10 each written in squares
- A primary pencil
- Scissors
- Construction paper to fit tray
- Glue stick

Setup:

1. Place three trays in a horizontal row
2. Place circle stencil and numerals in a container to the left of the first tray
3. **1st Tray:** Place white paper on tray and pencil on left side of tray
4. **2nd Tray:** Place scissors across the top of the tray
5. **3rd Tray:** Place colored paper on tray with a glue stick at the top of the tray

1st Tray

2nd Tray

Task:

1. **Beginning:** The goal is for the child to sort through numerals and find number 10 and trace that many circle shapes on the paper.
2. **Middle:** The goal is for the child to transfer the traced paper to the 2nd tray and cut out the shapes.
3. **End:** The goal is for the child to glue the shapes in two rows and glue the numeral square below the shape.

Outcome:

The child recognizes the number 10 and how many that number represents.

Emerging Skills:

The child develops numeral awareness and a sense of how many the numeral represents.

Extension Activity:

The following extension activity is presented as a challenge for the child who possesses an understanding of number symbols.

- Child writes the number to represent how many shapes are on the paper

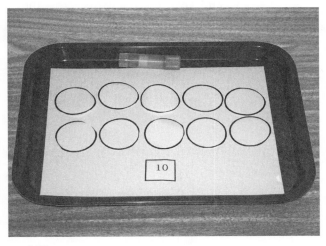

3rd Tray

SECTION VII—TRACE OR RUB USING CHALK, FOLD, CUT, AND GLUE

Task 55

Fold, Cut, and Glue

This section provides children with the opportunity to use chalk for tracing and drawing. It also encourages children to fold paper. White chalk and dark construction paper provides the recommended contrast so children can clearly see the results of their actions.

Materials:

- Three plastic rectangular trays
- Sheet of dark construction paper to fit tray
- White chalk
- Scissors
- Light colored construction paper to fit tray
- Glue stick

Setup:

1. Place three trays in a horizontal row
2. **1st Tray:** Place dark paper on tray with white chalk on left side of the tray
3. **2nd Tray:** Place scissors across the top of the tray
4. **3rd Tray:** Place colored sheet of construction paper with glue stick across the top of the tray

1st Tray

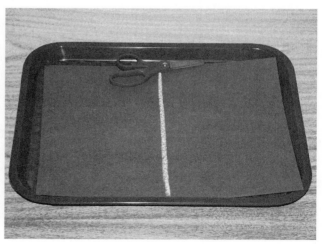

2nd Tray

⅜ Task:

1. **Beginning:** The goal is for the child to fold the dark construction paper one time, open, then draw a line on the fold with white chalk.
2. **Middle:** The goal is to transfer the dark construction paper to the 2nd tray and cut along the white chalk line.
3. **End:** The goal is to place the two pieces of dark construction paper on the light colored construction paper and glue back together again.

⅜ Outcome:

The child demonstrates his or her ability to fold and trace with chalk, then cut a straight line.

⅜ Emerging Skills:

The child refines his or her eye/hand coordination by using both hands in a coordinated motion to fold paper which strengthens his or her fine motor control.

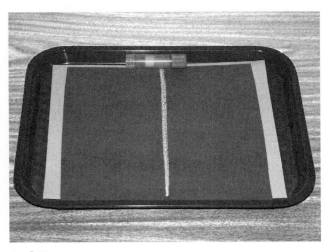

3rd Tray

Task 56

Multi-Fold, Cut, and Glue

⟫ Materials:

- Three plastic rectangular trays
- Sheet of dark construction paper to fit tray
- White chalk
- Scissors
- Light colored construction paper to fit tray
- Glue stick

⟫ Setup:

1. Place three trays in a horizontal row
2. **1st Tray:** Place dark paper on tray with white chalk on left side of the tray
3. **2nd Tray:** Place scissors across the top of the tray
4. **3rd Tray:** Place light colored construction paper on tray with glue stick across the top of the tray

1st Tray

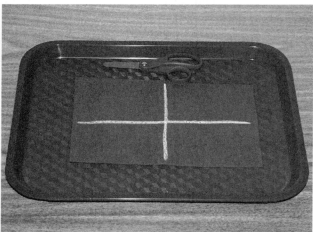

2nd Tray

⫸ *Task:*

1. **Beginning:** The goal is for the child to fold the dark construction paper in half, and then in half again. Open and lay flat, then trace the folds with white chalk.
2. **Middle:** The goal is for the child to transfer the paper to the 2nd tray and cut along the chalked fold lines.
3. **End:** The goal is to transfer the sections of dark paper to the 3rd tray and glue onto light construction paper so that the pieces fit on the paper.

⫸ *Outcome:*

The child increases his or her folding ability and drawing straight lines in the creases.

⫸ *Emerging Skills:*

The child develops multi-tasking and decision-making skills when assembling.

3rd Tray

Task 57

Rub, Cut, and Glue

))) Materials:

- Three plastic rectangular trays
- Sheet of white paper to fit tray
- One stencil made from recycled manila folder or poster board (it may be seasonal, theme related, or a shape)
- Colored chalk
- Scissors
- Construction paper to fit tray
- Glue stick

))) Setup:

1. Place three trays in a horizontal row
2. **1st Tray:** Tape the stencil to the tray and lay a sheet of white paper over the top, placing chalk on the left side of the tray.
3. **2nd Tray:** Place scissors across the top of the tray
4. **3rd Tray:** Place colored construction paper on tray and glue stick across the top of the tray

1st Tray

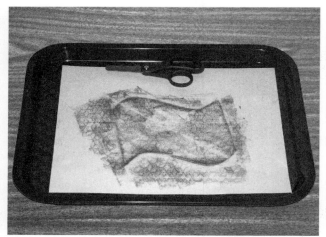

2nd Tray

 Task:

1. **Beginning:** The goal is for the child to lay a stick of colored chalk lengthwise on the paper and firmly rub back and forth to reveal an outline.
2. **Middle:** The goal is for the child to transfer the paper to the 2nd tray and cut out the revealed outline.
3. **End:** The goal is for the child to transfer the revealed outline onto the paper on the 3rd tray and glue.

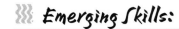 Outcome:

The child follows the sequence of steps to produce an outline.

Emerging Skills:

The child coordinates different hand motions at the same time while refining visual perception.

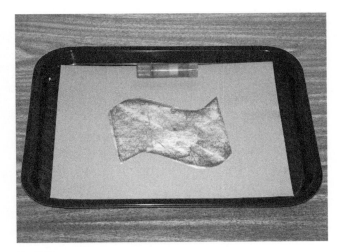

3rd Tray

Task 58

Trace, Cut, and Glue

))) Materials:

- Three plastic rectangular trays
- Dark construction paper to fit tray
- Crescent stencil
- White chalk
- Scissors
- White paper to fit tray
- Glue stick

))) Setup:

1. Place three trays in a horizontal row
2. **1st Tray:** Place sheet of dark paper on tray along with one piece of white chalk and crescent stencil
3. **2nd Tray:** Place scissors across the top of the tray
4. **3rd Tray:** Place white paper on 3rd tray with glue stick across the top of tray

1st Tray

2nd Tray

Task:

1. **Beginning:** The goal is for the child to position the stencil on the dark construction paper and trace around it with white chalk.
2. **Middle:** The goal is to transfer the paper to the 2nd tray and cut out with scissors.
3. **End:** The goal is to glue the cut out stencil onto a piece of white paper.

Outcome:

The child traces, cuts, and glues a shape onto paper using chalk.

Emerging Skills:

The child follows directions and proceeds from the beginning, to the middle, and finally to the end tray.

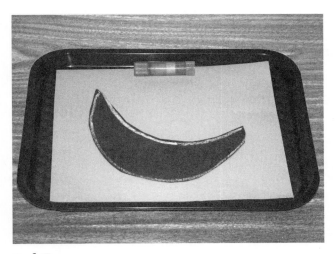

3rd Tray

Task 59

Parts Trace, Cut, and Glue

⦚ Materials:

- Three plastic rectangular trays
- Sheet of white paper to fit tray
- Colored chalk
- Stencil (any shape)
- Scissors
- Construction paper to fit tray
- Glue stick

⦚ Setup:

1. Place three trays in a horizontal row
2. **1st Tray:** Place white paper on tray with stencil. Put chalk on left side of tray.
3. **2nd Tray:** Place scissors across the top of the tray
4. **3rd Tray:** Place colored construction paper on tray and lay glue stick across the top of the tray

1st Tray

2nd Tray

Task:

1. **Beginning:** The goal is for the child to hold the stencil on the paper and trace using colored chalk.
2. **Middle:** The goal is to transfer the chalked outline to the 2nd tray and cut out with scissors, then cut the outline into several sections.
3. **End:** The goal is to reassemble the cut-out pieces on the colored construction paper.

Outcome:

The child moves through the sequence of trays to complete a project.

Emerging skills:

The child follows directions and refines grasp control while strengthening the wrist, hand, and finger muscles.

3rd Tray

Task 60

Inset Reverse, Cut, and Glue

⋙ Materials:

- Three plastic rectangular trays
- Sheet of white paper to fit tray
- Colored chalk
- Inset stencil
- Scissors
- Construction paper to fit tray
- Glue stick

⋙ Setup:

1. Place three trays in a horizontal row
2. **1st Tray:** Place white paper on tray with stencil, placing chalk to the left of tray
3. **2nd Tray:** Place scissors across the top of the tray
4. **3rd Tray:** Place colored construction paper on tray and place glue stick across the top of the tray

1st Tray

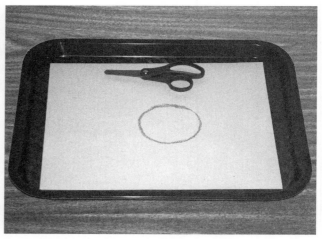

2nd Tray

Task:

1. **Beginning:** The goal is for the child to hold the inset and trace around the inside of it with colored chalk.
2. **Middle:** The goal is to transfer the completed inset tracing to the 2nd tray and cut out with scissors.
3. **End:** Glue the cut-out item on the 3rd tray, then color it using colored chalk.

Outcome:

The child is able to hold onto the inset and trace, cut, and color.

Emerging Skills:

The child is developing determination to complete a task.

3rd Tray

SECTION VIII—USING RULER, DRAW, CUT, AND GLUE

Task 61

Large Square— Draw, Cut, and Glue

The following tasks are provided for the older child who is able to hold a ruler and draw. These tasks provide children with an opportunity to multi-task and concentrate on controlling a pencil and ruler at the same time.

⅜ Materials:

- Three plastic rectangular trays
- White paper to fit tray
- Thin line marker
- Ruler (6 inches)
- Scissors
- Construction paper to fit tray
- Glue stick

⅜ Setup:

1. Place three trays in a horizontal row
2. **1st Tray:** Place white paper on tray with ruler and marker on the left side of tray
3. **2nd Tray:** Place scissors across top of tray
4. **3rd Tray:** Place colored paper on tray and glue stick across top of tray

1st Tray

2nd Tray

Task:

1. **Beginning:** The goal is for the child to select a color marker and use a ruler to draw a large square shape on the white paper.
2. **Middle:** The goal is to transfer the drawn shape to the 2nd tray and cut on the lines.
3. **End:** The goal is to place the cut-out shape on colored paper and glue into place.

Outcome:

The child successfully draws, cuts, and glues the shape created by using a ruler and a marker.

Emerging Skills:

The child successfully coordinates manipulation of a ruler and a pencil at the same time to create a square shape.

3rd Tray

Task 62

Small Square—Draw, Cut, and Glue

⌇⌇⌇ Materials:

- Three plastic rectangular trays
- White paper to fit tray
- Thin line marker
- Ruler (6 inches)
- Scissors
- Construction paper to fit tray
- Glue stick

⌇⌇⌇ Setup:

1. Place three trays in a horizontal row
2. **1st Tray:** Place white paper on tray and the ruler and marker on the left side of tray
3. **2nd Tray:** Place scissors across top of tray
4. **3rd Tray:** Place colored paper on tray and glue stick across top of tray

1st Tray

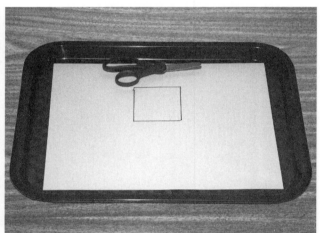

2nd Tray

Task:

1. **Beginning:** The goal is for the child to select the color marker and use a ruler to draw a small square shape on the white paper.
2. **Middle:** The goal is to transfer the drawn shape to the 2nd tray and then cut on the lines.
3. **End:** The goal is to place the cut-out shape on colored paper and glue into place.

Outcome:

The child successfully draws, cuts, and glues the shape created by using a ruler and a marker.

Emerging Skills:

The child manipulates a ruler and pencil accurately to create a small square shape.

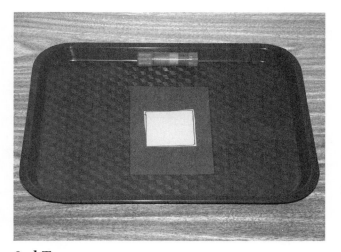

3rd Tray

Task 63

Large Rectangle— Draw, Cut, and Glue

※ Materials:

- Three plastic rectangular trays
- White paper to fit tray
- Thin line marker
- Ruler (6 inches)
- Scissors
- Construction paper to fit tray
- Glue stick

※ Setup:

1. Place three trays in a horizontal row
2. **1st Tray:** Place white paper on tray with ruler and marker on the left side of tray
3. **2nd Tray:** Place scissors across top of tray
4. **3rd Tray:** Place colored paper on tray and glue stick across top of tray

1st Tray

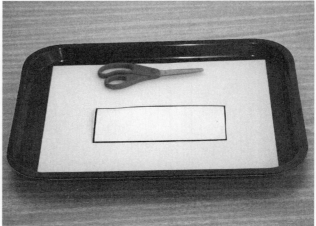

2nd Tray

Task:

1. **Beginning:** The goal is for the child to select the color marker and use a ruler to draw a large rectangle shape on the white paper.
2. **Middle:** The goal is to transfer the drawn shape to the 2nd tray and then cut on the lines.
3. **End:** The goal is to place cut-out shape on colored paper and glue into place.

Outcome:

The child successfully draws, cuts, and glues the shape created by using a ruler and a marker.

Emerging Skills:

The child is strengthening eye/hand coordination and muscle control when using a ruler and marker to attempt to create a specific shape.

3rd Tray

Task 64

Small Rectangle— Draw, Cut, and Glue

﷽ Materials:

- Three plastic rectangular trays
- White paper
- Thin line marker
- Ruler (6 inches)
- Scissors
- Construction paper to fit tray
- Glue stick

﷽ Setup:

1. Place three trays in a horizontal row
2. **1st Tray:** Place white paper on tray with ruler and marker on the left side of tray
3. **2nd Tray:** Place scissors across top of tray
4. **3rd Tray:** Place colored paper on tray and glue stick across top of tray

1st Tray

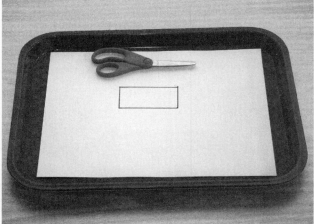

2nd Tray

Task:

1. **Beginning:** The goal is for the child to select the color marker and use a ruler to draw a small rectangle shape on the white paper.
2. **Middle:** The goal is to transfer the drawn shape to the 2nd tray and cut on the lines.
3. **End:** The goal is to place the cut-out shape on colored paper and glue into place.

Outcome:

The child successfully draws, cuts, and glues the shape created by using a ruler and a marker.

Emerging Skills:

The child is determining size when drawing the shape with a ruler and marker.

3rd Tray

Task 65

Large Triangle— Draw, Cut, and Glue

Materials:

- Three plastic rectangular trays
- White paper to fit tray
- Large triangle stencil
- Thin line marker
- Ruler (6 inches)
- Scissors
- Construction paper to fit tray
- Glue stick

Setup:

1. Place three trays in a horizontal row
2. **1st Tray:** Place white paper on tray. Place large triangle stencil on paper. Position ruler and thin line marker on the left side of tray
3. **2nd Tray:** Place scissors across top of tray
4. **3rd Tray:** Place colored paper on tray and glue stick across top of tray

1st Tray

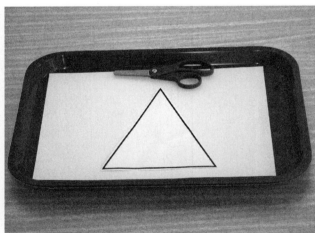

2nd Tray

◊◊◊ *Task:*

1. **Beginning:** The goal is for the child to use a thin line marker and a ruler to draw a large triangle.
2. **Middle:** The goal is to transfer the large triangle to the 2nd tray and cut on the lines.
3. **End:** The goal is to place the cut-out triangle on colored paper and glue into place.

◊◊◊ *Outcome:*

The child successfully draws, cuts, and glues the shape created by using a ruler and a marker.

◊◊◊ *Emerging Skills:*

The child utilizes visual discrimination to determine the size of the shape while manipulating a ruler and marker.

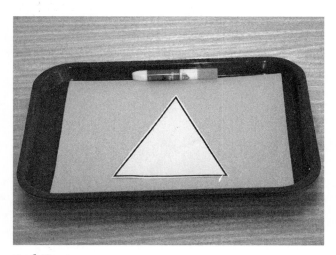

3rd Tray

Task 66

Small Triangle— Draw, Cut, and Glue

░ Materials:

- Three plastic rectangular trays
- White paper to fit tray
- Thin line marker
- Ruler (6 inches)
- Scissors
- Construction paper to fit tray
- Glue stick

░ Setup:

1. Place three trays in a horizontal row
2. **1st Tray:** Place white paper on tray with ruler and marker on the left side of tray
3. **2nd Tray:** Place scissors across top of tray
4. **3rd Tray:** Place colored paper on tray and glue stick across top of tray

1st Tray

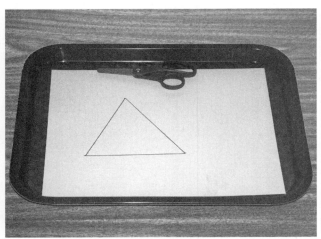

2nd Tray

Task:

1. **Beginning:** The goal is for the child to use a thin line marker and a ruler to draw a small triangle shape on the white paper.
2. **Middle:** The goal is to transfer the drawn shape to the 2nd tray and cut on the lines.
3. **End:** The goal is to place the cut-out shape on colored paper and glue into place.

Outcome:

The child successfully draws, cuts, and glues the shape created by using a ruler and a marker.

Emerging Skills:

The child determines the size of the triangle when creating it on paper using the ruler and marker.

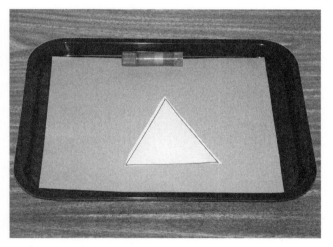

3rd Tray

Task 67

Large Diamond— Draw, Cut, and Glue

⁂ Materials:

- Three plastic rectangular trays
- Sheet of white paper to fit tray
- Thin line marker
- Ruler (6 inches)
- Scissors
- Construction paper to fit tray
- Glue stick

⁂ Setup:

1. Place three trays in a horizontal row
2. **1st Tray:** Place white paper on tray and ruler and marker on left side of tray
3. **2nd Tray:** Place scissors across top of tray
4. **3rd Tray:** Place colored paper on tray and glue stick across top of tray

1st Tray

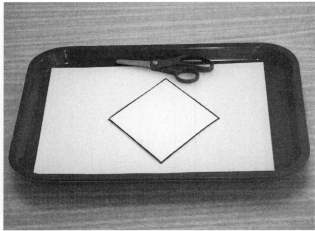

2nd Tray

⫶⫶ Task:

1. **Beginning:** The goal is for the child to use a thin line marker and a ruler to draw a large diamond shape on the white paper.

2. **Middle:** The goal is to transfer the drawn shape to the 2nd tray and cut on the lines.

3. **End:** The goal is to place the cut-out shape on colored paper and glue into place.

⫶⫶ Outcome:

The child successfully draws, cuts, and glues the shape created by using a ruler and a marker.

⫶⫶ Emerging Skills:

The child is able to determine the size of the diamond shape before beginning to attempt to create it using a ruler and marker.

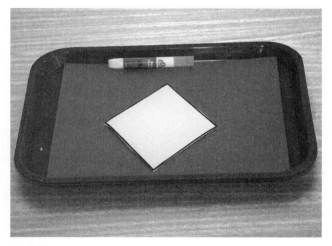

3rd Tray

Task 68

Small Diamond— Draw, Cut, and Glue

▒ Materials:

- Three plastic rectangular trays
- Sheet of white paper to fit tray
- Thin line marker
- Ruler (6 inches)
- Scissors
- Construction paper to fit tray
- Glue stick

▒ Setup:

1. Place three trays in a horizontal row
2. **1st Tray:** Place white paper on tray and put marker and ruler on the left side of tray
3. **2nd Tray:** Place scissors across top of tray
4. **3rd Tray:** Place colored paper on tray and glue stick across top of tray

1st Tray

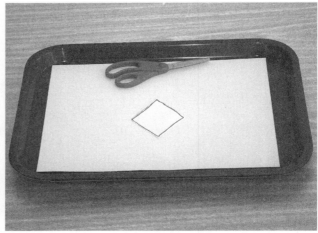

2nd Tray

Task:

1. **Beginning:** The goal is for the child to use a thin line marker and a ruler to draw a small diamond shape on the white paper.
2. **Middle:** The goal is to transfer the drawn shape to the 2nd tray and cut on the lines.
3. **End:** The goal is to place the cut-out shape on colored paper and glue into place.

 ## Outcome:

The child successfully draws, cuts, and glues the shape created by using a ruler and a marker.

Emerging Skills:

The child is able to determine the size of a small diamond shape before using the ruler and marker.

3rd Tray

Task 69

Large Pentagon— Draw, Cut, and Glue

))) *Materials:*

- Three plastic rectangular trays
- White paper to fit tray
- Thin line marker
- Ruler (6 inches)
- Scissors
- Construction paper to fit tray
- Glue stick

))) *Setup:*

1. Place three trays in a horizontal row
2. **1st Tray:** Place white paper, marker, and ruler on tray
3. **2nd Tray:** Place scissors across top of tray
4. **3rd Tray:** Place construction paper on tray and glue stick across top of tray

1st Tray

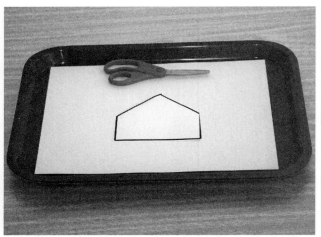

2nd Tray

Task:

1. **Beginning:** The goal is for the child to use a thin line marker and a ruler to draw a large pentagon shape on the white paper.
2. **Middle:** The goal is to transfer the drawn shape to the 2nd tray and cut on the lines.
3. **End:** The goal is to place the cut-out shape on colored paper and glue into place.

Outcome:

The child successfully draws, cuts, and glues the large pentagon shape created by using a ruler and a marker.

Emerging Skills:

The child attempts to use a ruler and marker to draw a large pentagon shape on paper.

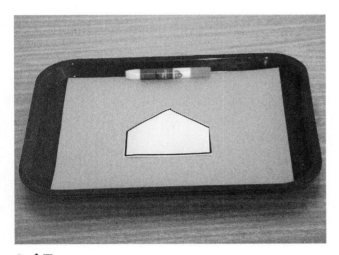

3rd Tray

Task 70

Small Pentagon— Draw, Cut, and Glue

Materials:

- Three plastic rectangular trays
- White paper to fit tray
- Thin line marker
- Ruler (6 inches)
- Scissors
- Construction paper to fit tray
- Glue stick

Setup:

1. Place three trays in a horizontal row
2. **1st Tray:** Place white paper, marker, and ruler on tray
3. **2nd Tray:** Place scissors across top of tray
4. **3rd Tray:** Place construction paper on tray and glue stick across top of tray

1st Tray

2nd Tray

Task:

1. **Beginning:** The goal is for the child to use a thin line marker and a ruler to draw a small pentagon shape on the white paper.
2. **Middle:** The goal is to transfer the drawn shape to the 2nd tray and cut on the lines.
3. **End:** The goal is to place the cut-out shape on colored paper and glue into place.

Outcome:

The child successfully draws, cuts, and glues the small pentagon shape created by using a ruler and a marker.

Emerging Skills:

The child is developing a sense of proportion when determining how to construct a small pentagon shape on paper using a ruler and marker.

3rd Tray

Task 71

Multi-Lines, Cut, and Glue

《 Materials:

- Three plastic rectangular trays
- White paper to fit tray
- Thick line marker
- Ruler (6 inches)
- Scissors
- Construction paper to fit tray
- Glue stick

《 Setup:

1. Place three trays in a horizontal row
2. **1st Tray:** Place white paper, marker, and ruler on tray
3. **2nd Tray:** Place scissors across top of tray
4. **3rd Tray:** Place construction paper on tray and glue stick across top of tray

1st Tray

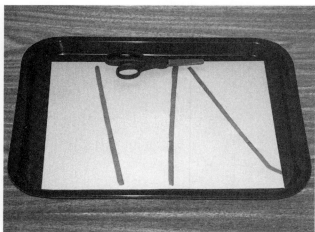

2nd Tray

⧚ *Task:*

1. **Beginning:** The goal is for the child to use a thick line marker and a ruler to make a series of thick lines drawing from top to bottom of the paper.
2. **Middle:** The goal is to move the paper to the cutting tray and cut along the side of each line creating strips of paper lines.
3. **End:** The goal is to transfer cut strips onto the next tray and glue into any desired position on the paper.

⧚ *Outcome:*

The child applies creative choice to design gluing positions of strips onto paper.

⧚ *Emerging Skills:*

The child advances his or her ability to multi-task, use a ruler, and draw with a thick marker to create the finished task.

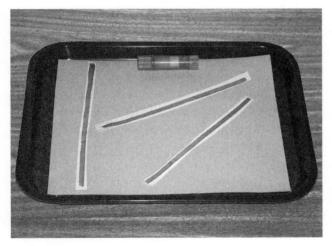

3rd Tray

Task 72

Length Seriating, Cut, and Glue

⅏ Materials:

- Three plastic rectangular trays
- White paper to fit tray
- Three different colors of thick line markers
- Ruler (6 inches)
- Scissors
- Construction paper to fit tray
- Glue stick

⅏ Setup:

1. Place three trays in a horizontal row
2. **1st Tray:** Place white paper, markers, and ruler on tray
3. **2nd Tray:** Place scissors across top of tray
4. **3rd Tray:** Place construction paper on tray and glue stick across top of tray

1st Tray

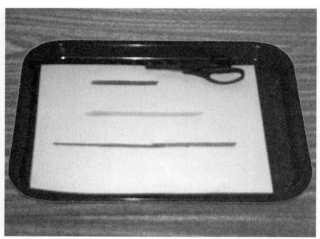

2nd Tray

Task:

1. **Beginning:** The goal is for the child to select one marker at a time and use a ruler to make thick lines in three different lengths. Use a different color marker for each line.

2. **Middle:** The goal is to move the paper to the cutting tray and cut along the sides of each line to create strips of paper lines in varying lengths.

3. **End:** The goal is to transfer cut strips onto the next tray and glue starting with the shortest length first across the top of the paper. Then, glue the midsized length, and so on until all are glued showing differences in length.

Outcome:

The child successfully problem solves how to position strip lengths from the shortest length to the longest on the final paper.

Emerging Skills:

The child uses problem-solving skills to determine how to draw, cut, and glue three lengths of strips on paper.

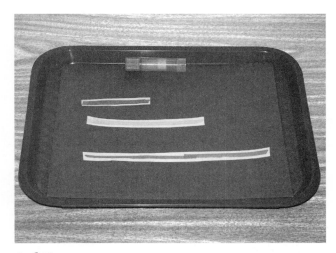

3rd Tray

Task 73

Height Seriating, Cut, and Glue

⚜ Materials:

- Three plastic rectangular trays
- White paper to fit tray
- Three different colors of thick line markers
- Ruler (6 inches)
- Scissors
- Construction paper to fit tray
- Glue stick

⚜ Setup:

1. Place three trays in a horizontal row
2. **1st Tray:** Place white paper, markers, and ruler on tray
3. **2nd Tray:** Place scissors across top of tray
4. **3rd Tray:** Place construction paper on tray and glue stick across top of tray

1st Tray

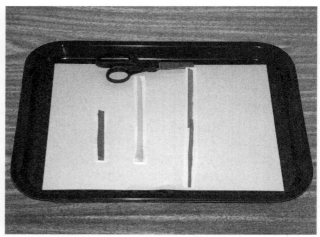

2nd Tray

⣿ *Task:*

1. **Beginning:** The goal is for the child to select one marker at a time and use a ruler to make thick lines in three different heights, starting at the top of the paper toward the bottom. Use a different color marker for each line.

2. **Middle:** The goal is to move the paper to the cutting tray and cut along the sides of each thick line to make paper strips of varying heights.

3. **End:** The goal is to transfer cut strips onto the next tray and glue in a seriating order from the shortest to the tallest line starting at the left side of the paper.

⣿ *Outcome:*

The child successfully seriates paper strips while gluing the strips from shortest to tallest lines.

⣿ *Emerging Skills:*

The child uses his or her thinking skills to determine how to draw different heights of lines to accommodate this task.

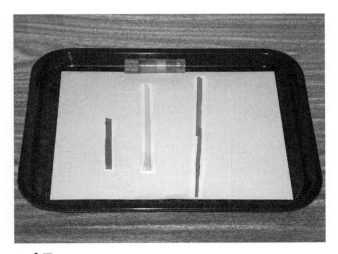

3rd Tray

Task 74

Left-to-Right Lines, Cut, and Glue

))) Materials:

- Three plastic rectangular trays
- White paper to fit tray
- Three different colors of thick line markers
- Ruler (6 inches)
- Scissors
- Construction paper to fit tray
- Glue stick

))) Setup:

1. Place three trays in a horizontal row
2. **1st Tray:** Place white paper, markers, and ruler on tray
3. **2nd Tray:** Place scissors across top of tray
4. **3rd Tray:** Place construction paper on tray and glue stick across top of tray

1st Tray

2nd Tray

 Task:

1. **Beginning:** The goal is for the child to select one marker at a time and use a ruler to make three thick vertical lines drawing from the left side of the paper to the right side of the paper. Use a different color marker for each line.

2. **Middle:** The goal is to move the paper to the cutting tray and cut along the sides of each thick line creating paper strips.

3. **End:** The goal is to transfer cut strips onto the next tray and glue onto the paper to create vertical lines from left to right across the paper.

Outcome:

The child successfully applies left-to-right directionality while gluing paper.

Emerging Skills:

This task requires problem solving and concentrated thinking skills to determine the use of the three markers needed to make three lines and assembling them into vertical left-to-right positions when gluing onto the paper.

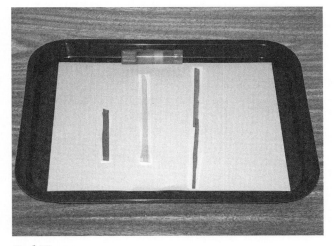

3rd Tray

SECTION IX—ORGANIZING AND ASSEMBLING BOOKLETS

Task 75

Alphabet Booklet

In this section, we are inviting children to create booklets. Practice using a single hole punch should be given prior to the tray task. Opportunities should also be provided for children to practice threading yarn or ribbon in and out of holes to create a binding for booklets. A three hole punch may also be introduced as another way to create holes on the left side of paper to create booklets. A hole punching and threading area may be established as an extension of your art or small manipulative area for these actions. A basket or container may be used to house a hole punch, yarn, ribbon, and paper for children to choose as an activity in the art area.

It is recommended that children create a cover page and place his or her name on each booklet. This builds self-esteem and establishes the child as the author of the work.

Materials:

- Three plastic rectangular trays
- White paper to fit tray (several)
- A primary pencil
- Uppercase and lowercase letters of the whole alphabet
- Scissors
- 13 sheets of 4″ × 6″ colored construction paper
- Glue stick
- Single hole punch
- Yarn or ribbon

Setup:

1. Place three trays in a horizontal row
2. **1st Tray:** Place one sheet of white paper on tray and place pencil across the top of the tray. Place letters to the side of the tray.
3. **2nd Tray:** Place scissors across the top of the tray
4. **3rd Tray:** Place colored paper on tray with a glue stick at the top of the tray and hole punch to the side of the tray with yarn

1st Tray

2nd Tray

Task:

1. **Beginning:** The goal is for the child to sort through letters and find an uppercase and lowercase letter that matches, and trace them on the paper. This task extends over several days in order to trace and cut all 26 uppercase and lowercase letters.

2. **Middle:** The goal is for the child to transfer the traced paper to the 2nd tray and cut out the letters.

3. **End:** The goal is for the child to glue the matched uppercase and lowercase letters onto the appropriate front and back of construction paper to read like a book. Then, punch holes down the left side of pages. After completing all 26 uppercase and lowercase letters, the child binds the pages together with yarn.

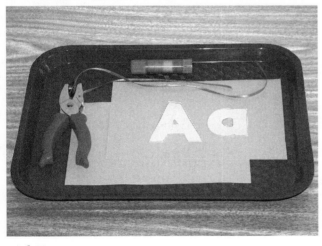

3rd Tray

Outcome:

The child recognizes uppercase and lowercase alphabet letters and places them in an alphabetical ordering on the pages of the booklet.

Emerging Skills:

The child develops an awareness of letters and a sense of alphabetic principle. He or she uses sequencing skills to organize pages into a booklet.

Extension Activity:

The following extension activities are presented as a challenge for the child who possesses ability for letter recognition and letter formations.

- Child writes each page's uppercase and lowercase letters over an extended period of days
- Child draws a picture or writes a word that begins with each letter on every page

Task 76

Number Booklet

⁘ *Materials:*

- Three plastic rectangular trays
- White paper with ten squares
- A primary pencil
- Scissors
- 10 sheets of 4″ × 6″ construction paper
- Glue stick
- Single hole punch
- Yarn or ribbon

⁘ *Setup:*

1. Place three trays in a horizontal row
2. **1st Tray:** Place white paper filled with ten squares on tray and place pencil on the left side of the tray
3. **2nd Tray:** Place scissors across the top of the tray
4. **3rd Tray:** Place colored paper on tray with a glue stick at the top of the tray and hole punch to the side of the tray with yarn or ribbon

1st Tray

2nd Tray

Task:

1. **Beginning:** The goal is for the child to write numbers 1–10 with one numeral in each square.
2. **Middle:** The goal is for the child to transfer the traced paper to the 2nd tray and cut out the numeral squares.
3. **End:** The goal is for the child to glue the numeral squares in sequence from 1–10 on individual sheets of construction paper. Then, the child should punch holes down the left side of pages and bind them together with yarn to form a booklet.

Outcome:

The child is using counting skills and ordering numbers from 1–10 on the pages of the booklet.

Emerging Skills:

The child is developing numeral awareness skills and is associating the order of counting with the number squares to organize the pages into a booklet.

Extension Activity:

The following extension activity is presented as a challenge for the child who possesses ability for number recognition.

● Ask child to draw objects on each page to represent each number in the booklet

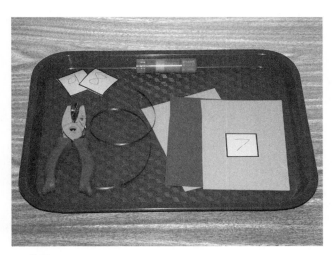

3rd Tray

Task 77

Parts-to-a-Whole Booklet

This task is for older children who have an understanding of fractions and the ability to section circles into equal parts with a ruler.

Materials:

- Three plastic rectangular trays
- Small container to hold fraction labels
- A sheet of white paper with five circles drawn on the page
- A primary pencil
- Ruler
- Five half-sheets construction paper
- Glue stick
- Fraction labels 1/2, 1/3, 1/4, 1/5, and 1
- Single hole punch
- Yarn or ribbon

Setup:

1. Place three trays in a horizontal row
2. **1st Tray:** Place white paper with drawn circles on tray and place pencil and ruler on the left side of the tray
3. **2nd Tray:** Place scissors across the top of the tray
4. **3rd Tray:** Place five half-sheets of colored paper on tray with a glue stick at the top of the tray and hole punch on side of tray with yarn or ribbon

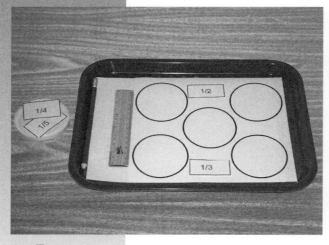

1st Tray

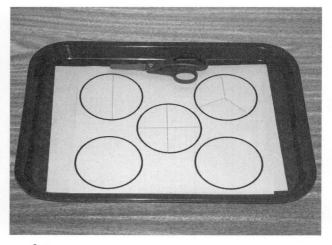

2nd Tray

⦚ *Task:*

1. **Beginning:** The goal is for the child to use a ruler and pencil to section four circles into 2 equal parts, 3 equal parts, 4 equal parts and 5 equal parts. (One circle will remain empty as it will represent 1, or a whole).

2. **Middle:** The goal is for the child to transfer the traced paper to the 2nd tray and cut out the circle shapes.

3. **End:** The goal is for the child to glue each circle to a separate sheet of construction paper and glue the matching fraction labels below each circle. Punch holes down the left side of the pages and bind with yarn to create a parts-to-a-whole booklet.

⦚ *Outcome:*

The child demonstrates the understanding of parts to a whole and fraction concepts.

⦚ *Emerging Skills:*

The child is developing fraction awareness.

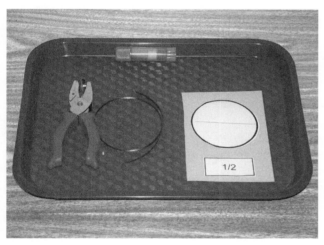

3rd Tray

Task 78

Sequencing Booklet

Materials:

- Three plastic rectangular trays
- Sheet of white paper to fit tray
- A primary pencil
- Small square, triangle, and diamond stencils
- Scissors
- Three half-sheets of construction paper
- Glue stick
- Single hole punch
- Yarn or ribbon

Setup:

1. Place three trays in a horizontal row
2. **1st Tray:** Place white paper on tray. Place pencil on the left side of tray. Place square, triangle, and diamond stencils on white paper
3. **2nd Tray:** Place scissors across the top of the tray
4. **3rd Tray:** Place three half-sheets of colored paper on tray with a glue stick across the top of the tray and single hole punch on side of tray with yarn

1st Tray

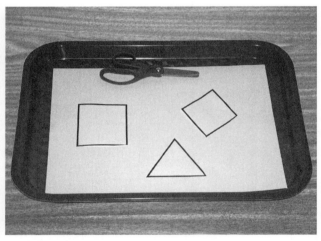

2nd Tray

Task:

1. **Beginning:** The goal is for the child to trace each of the shapes onto the white paper.
2. **Middle:** The goal is for the child to transfer the traced paper to the 2nd tray and cut out the shapes.
3. **End:** The goal is for the child to glue one shape per page, then place pages in order of square, triangle, and then diamond. The child is to hole punch pages, and bind with yarn.

Outcome:

The child sequences shapes according to the order of square, triangle, diamond.

Emerging Skills:

The child is practicing sequence skills to organize pages into a booklet.

Extension Activity:

As an extension activity, have children glue labels on each page with ordinal numbers and shape word labels. Ordinal labels are 1st, 2nd, and 3rd. Shape word labels are square, triangle, and diamond.

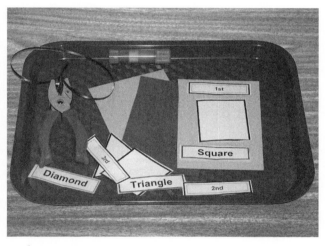

3rd Tray

Task 79

Shape Booklet

≋ Materials:

- Three plastic rectangular trays
- White paper with five half-drawn shapes: square, rectangle, triangle, circle, diamond
- Thin line marker
- Scissors
- Five half-sheets of construction paper
- Glue stick
- Single hole punch
- Yarn or ribbon

≋ Setup:

1. Place three trays in a horizontal row
2. **1st Tray:** Place white paper with half-drawn shapes and marker on tray
3. **2nd Tray:** Place scissors across the top of the tray
4. **3rd Tray:** Place construction paper on tray with a glue stick at the top of the tray and single hole punch on side of tray with yarn

1st Tray

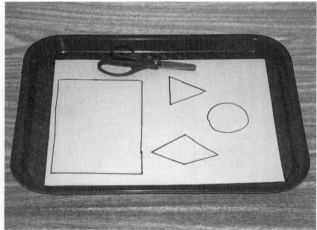

2nd Tray

Task:

1. **Beginning:** The goal is for the child to use the marker to complete the drawing of each of the shapes.
2. **Middle:** The goal is for the child to transfer the traced paper to the 2nd tray and cut out the shapes.
3. **End:** The goal is for the child to glue each shape onto a sheet of colored construction paper in the order of circle, diamond, rectangle, square, and triangle. Then, the child will punch holes down the left side of each sheet of paper and bind with yarn.

Outcome:

The child attempts to free-hand draw the completed shapes and organize into a booklet format following the order given.

Emerging Skills:

The child uses his or her visual perception ability to complete the partially drawn shapes and organize the booklet.

Extension Activity:

For the older child, word labels to identify each shape may be added to glue onto the appropriate page.

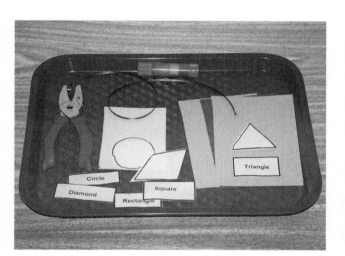

3rd Tray

Task 80

Size Booklet

⧓ Materials:

- Three plastic rectangular trays
- Small container to hold stencils
- White paper to fit tray
- Small, medium, and large stencils of two shapes: hearts and squares
- Thin line marker
- Scissors
- Half-sheets of construction paper
- Glue stick
- Single hole punch
- Yarn or ribbon

⧓ Setup:

1. Place three trays in a horizontal row
2. Place six heart and square stencils of each size in a small container
3. **1st Tray:** Place white paper and marker on tray
4. **2nd Tray:** Place scissors across the top of the tray
5. **3rd Tray:** Place half-sheets of construction paper on tray with a glue stick at the top of the tray and place hole punch on side of tray with yarn or ribbon

1st Tray

2nd Tray

⫸ *Task:*

1. **Beginning:** The goal is for the child to trace a small, medium, and large size of each of the two shapes.
2. **Middle:** The goal is for the child to transfer the traced papers to the 2nd tray and cut out the shapes.
3. **End:** The goal is for the child to glue the shapes according to the following sequence:
   - 1 side of a page—small and medium size of one shape
   - 1 side of facing page—large size of same shape
   - Encourage child to use front and back of pages
   - Repeat the order for both shapes
   - Punch holes down the left side of the pages and bind all pages with yarn to create a booklet

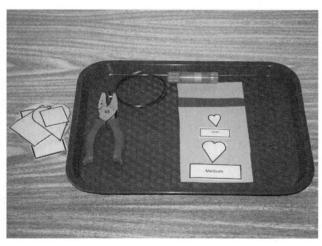

3rd Tray

⫸ *Outcome:*

The child demonstrates the ability to follow directions and organize the booklet according to the given directions.

⫸ *Emerging Skills:*

The child is developing an awareness of the different attributes of shapes.

⫸ *Extension Activity:*

The following extension activity is presented as a challenge for the child who possesses an understanding of identifying word labels and correctly matching them to shapes.

- Child glues word labels (small, medium, and large) that match each shape size